ADVANCE PRAISE FOR *SPECIAL TOPICS IN BEING A PARENT*

"*Special Topics in Being a Parent* encourages you to meet your children with the same kind of bravery, honesty, curiosity, and joy that you hope they will carry with them throughout their lives. Full of encouragement, compassion, and practical tips, it is the perfect resource for imperfect parents who are ready to let go of the need to constantly optimize themselves and their kids and to embrace all that is weird and wonderful."
–Jennifer Peepas, writer of CaptainAwkward.com

"S. Bear Bergman has done it again–this time with a book about the challenging task of raising more ethical, more loving kids (and their parents). *Special Topics in Being a Parent* is infused with wisdom, wry humour, and most importantly, a wealth of actionable, genuinely novel tips and tricks for getting through parenthood with more wholeness, more joy, more love. I so wish I'd had this book when my kids were younger, but since I'm not done parenting, I'm not done needing this."
–Rabbi Danya Ruttenberg, author of *Nurture the Wow* and *On Repentance and Repair*

"*Special Topics in Being a Parent* is an honest, humorous, sincere, and powerful guide for parenting. As a queer parent myself, I found this book to be so relatable. The stunning illustrations by Saul Freedman-Lawson complement the text wonderfully. This is one of my favourite new books, and I recommend it to every parent out there."
–Hasan Namir, author of *Umbilical Cord* and *Banana Dream*

SPECIAL TOPICS
IN BEING A
PARENT

A QUEER AND TENDER GUIDE TO
THINGS I'VE LEARNED ABOUT PARENTING,
MOSTLY THE HARD WAY

S. BEAR BERGMAN
ILLUSTRATED BY SAUL FREEDMAN-LAWSON

ARSENAL PULP PRESS
VANCOUVER

ARSENAL PULP PRESS
Suite 202 – 211 East Georgia St.
Vancouver, BC V6A 1Z6
Canada
arsenalpulp.com

The publisher gratefully acknowledges the support of the Canada Council for the Arts and the British Columbia Arts Council for its publishing program and the Government of Canada and the Government of British Columbia (through the Book Publishing Tax Credit Program) for its publishing activities.

Arsenal Pulp Press acknowledges the xʷməθkʷəy̓əm (Musqueam), Sḵwx̱wú7mesh (Squamish), and səlilwətaɬ (Tsleil-Waututh) Nations, custodians of the traditional, ancestral, and unceded territories where our office is located. We pay respect to their histories, traditions, and continuous living cultures and commit to accountability, respectful relations, and friendship.

Cover design by Saul Freedman-Lawson
Edited by Catharine Chen
Proofread by JC Cham

Printed and bound in Korea

Library and Archives Canada Cataloguing in Publication:
Title: Special topics in being a parent : a queer and tender guide to things I've learned about parenting, mostly the hard way / S. Bear Bergman ; illustrated by Saul Freedman-Lawson.
Names: Bergman, S. Bear, 1974– author. | Freedman-Lawson, Saul, illustrator.
Identifiers: Canadiana (print) 20230538576 | Canadiana (ebook) 20230538606 | ISBN 9781551529394 (softcover) | ISBN 9781551529400 (EPUB)
Subjects: LCSH: Bergman, S. Bear, 1974- | LCSH: Parenting—Anecdotes. | LCSH: Parenting—Humor. | LCSH: Child rearing—Anecdotes. | LCSH: Child rearing—Humor.
Classification: LCC HQ755.8 .B47 2024 | DDC 649/.10207—dc23

This book is dedicated to my husband, co-parent, collaborator, and sweetheart, j wallace skelton.

—SBB

For parents (especially my mother and father) and children (especially of my family) and the people who love them (especially myself).

—SFL

Contents

I was a perfect parent
before I had actual
children.

For quite some time, I would have told you that I did not want children of my own.

I'm a queer person who came out young for my time—in 1990 not many sixteen-year-olds were out—and that, combined with my predisposition toward wanting to be helpful under absolutely any circumstances, meant that I spent years being cast, very willingly, as a sort of community dad.

Did I have the skills for this? No. Was I emotionally or spiritually ready to do that work? Absolutely not—I was still years away from starting work on my own business. I had, at best, about three shreds of information, a couple of older queer friends, and a tiny amount of experience in queer community spaces, most of them online. Plus I read a lot.

But I responded strongly to the needs of the people around me who were lost and scared and flailing miserably.

I tried to help as best I could, but I was functionally the equivalent of a brand-new teacher who is one chapter ahead of his students in the book they're all reading: I could only see over the next hill.

I didn't have any context,

just my imagining of how things were supposed to go

and the slenderest fraction more of a clue than the people around me, on a good day.

I often felt exhausted and overwhelmed by the needs people brought to me, but I had no way to talk about that. I think overall I did more good than harm, but that calculus never feels as solid as I would prefer.

Eventually I met the man I would marry,

who already had one older child (of whom he shared custody)

and dearly wanted more.

I was besotted by his brains

and his sentence structure,

his deep care and kindness

(not to mention his handsome face and superlative backside).

He said that he was actively making plans to have a baby and that if I was going to be around I should know that up front. I said—after years of telling anyone who would listen that I was already spending a lot of my time undoing bad parenting and wasn't really interested in adding to the amount of it in the world—yes. I said that I was in.

Thereupon I began a private program of readying myself to be the father I wanted to be:

caring and connected,

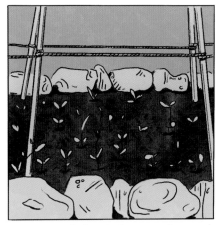

engaged but boundaried,

ready to give a child a stable frame upon which
to grow and be well.

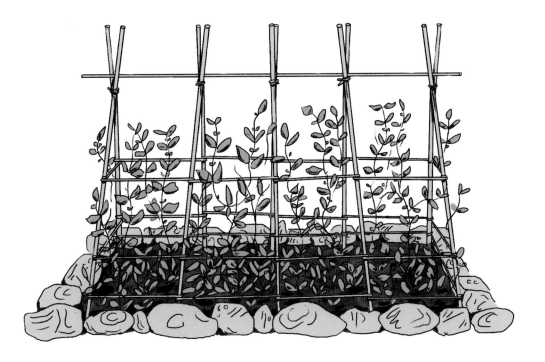

I imagined hundreds, if not thousands, of conversations in which I responded to imagined issues in parenting. In the car as I drove, or while I walked and thought my little thoughts,

I explained things,

...AND SO THE REASON THAT BUTTERFLY IS TWO COLOURS IS CALLED BILATERAL GYNANDROMORPHISM...

set limits,

HOW CAN WE MAKE SURE EVERYONE GETS A TURN?

WE COULD SET A TIMER?

GOOD IDEA!

CAN I HAVE THE REST OF THE GARLIC TOFU?

YOU MAY HAVE SECONDS OF GARLIC TOFU ONCE EVERYONE ELSE HAS HAD FIRSTS.

made agreements,

I HEAR THAT YOU ARE UPSET, AND THAT MAKES SENSE. CAN WE TAKE SOME DEEP BREATHS TOGETHER TO HELP US BOTH FEEL CALM?

and rehearsed all sorts of measured and thoughtful responses to all sorts of parenting issues.

My imaginary child responded thoughtfully to my wise counsel, and every conversation ended with a hug.

(And not, say, the child starting to hum tunelessly and wander off four seconds into my carefully crafted monologue.)

This child was creative

but never destructive,

suspicious about authority

but never questioned mine,

and they felt a freedom to be whomever in the world, in exactly the ways I had yearned to feel free but never was.

The astute reader will already have noticed a possible issue here.

The truth, I discovered, is that being a parent requires a very different set of skills and preparation than I could possibly have imagined. Also, children are all very different—both from my imagination and from one another—so what works on one may or may not work on another. Beyond all of that, I was busy preparing for situations like a kid going to a party and getting drunk,

which not at all coincidentally was the kind of community parenting I had already been doing. It wasn't unhelpful, but there are rather a lot of other things that crop up first, like

WHY DO YOU WAKE UP AT 5:30 A.M. AND SCREAM FOR NO DISCERNIBLE REASON UNTIL SOMEONE TAKES YOU OUT FOR A WALK?

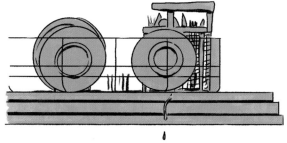

HOW ON EARTH DO YOU LOSE ONE SHOE?

WHY DID YOU PEE IN THE DISHWASHER?

I will save you the trouble and reveal that the answer to all such queries, if any, is always

I DON'T KNOW

which is somehow the worst, because it leaves you nowhere to go. There's no sense to question, no decision-making point at which you can usefully intervene.

Argh.

PRO TIP:

Questions are always a crapshoot. For example, you may think at some point that it's a good idea to ask your child

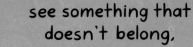

WHAT IS IN YOUR SHOES?

reasonably anticipating that they'll peer in, see a pound of sand or three rocks or a handful of Lego, be immediately contrite, and repatriate the items appropriately. What will actually happen is that they'll

peer in,

see something that doesn't belong,

then promptly turn their shoe over and dump the contents all over the floor.

So now I am done making new babies, and I have made my way through many stages of parenting with several excellent children and figured out a few things through trial and error,

but let's be honest: mostly error.

My preparations never took into account that

I would be completely exhausted

or that someone else would be shrieking

or that I would already have said the same thing one hundred thousand times

or that the behaviour would be okay,

but the timing terrible

I DO WANT A HUG, BUT WHEN I AM FINISHED POOPING, PLEASE

or any of the many, many other things one is forced to learn when one has actual children rather than the fictional, imagined children in our heads.

More effective preparation for parenting would have been going to Grand Central Terminal with an heirloom vase in one hand and trying to apply shoes to an octopus while a team of middle schoolers threw tennis balls at my head and a countdown clock screamed the time at me every five seconds.

What I have noticed, however, as of this writing—with children who are twenty-eight, thirteen, and eight—is that I am managing to put a few things together, in retrospect.

THE OCTOPUS DOES NOT NEED SHOES.

It's tremendously inconvenient because most of this would have been much more useful beforehand rather than after, but such is the way of parenting.

ONE IS ALWAYS

to quote my still-very-smart-and-also-good-looking husband,

READY FOR LAST WEEK'S CHILD

the child you no longer have because they have already grown and morphed and have a new

need

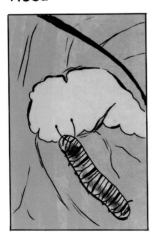

or phase

or experience

to respond to.

The learning curve is steep,

and you will be surfing
it most of the time,

which is actually a splendid metaphor:

there's a lot of getting up
very early,

a lot of hard work
paddling,

the great and joyful golden moments when you're up and
on the wave and it feels like you're holy shit doing the
thing for real and it's perfect and amazing,

and then getting dumped
out of that moment

and tumbled around like
you're in a washing machine

and sometimes held under far longer
than you feel you can manage,

plus you end up with
weird injuries you
can't recall getting,

and somehow there is
always sand everywhere.

Also many things become clear only in retrospect. I was reminded of this fact just last week, when I casually replied to McSweeney's editor Lucy Huber's tweet about her son never ever wanting to sleep later than 5:30 a.m. to say that

SOME GROW OUT OF IT, BUT IF NOT, TEACH THEM TO BAKE

—and was flooded by replies acclaiming my genius.

Friends, listen: I absolutely did not plan for that. I am not remotely that smart. I figured it out when one of our non-sleeping children started getting up early and decided to bake something since they were barred from weekend iPad use until 7:30 a.m.

following several instances of finding that child hunched over their device at 5 a.m. like it was the signal fire keeping their hope of rescue alive.

<u>Ten years later</u> I figured out that these things go well together (and also that children of eightish can definitely make hand pies in a muffin tin with scratch crust by themselves if they want to, and also also that baking is safer from a fire-risk standpoint than stovetop cookery).

And so, at this point in parenting—

both the ad hoc, ex post papa kind that I started rather early on, and the immediate and relentless kind that I do now with the children for whom I am directly and everlastingly responsible— I have learned a few things.

Some of them in retrospect, mostly through making mistakes and trying to fix them,

a considerable number from my actual, non-imaginary children,

and a tiny precious few through having had an actual good idea.

I've learned that it's
fine to be a cool dad
and let your kid play
with flour,

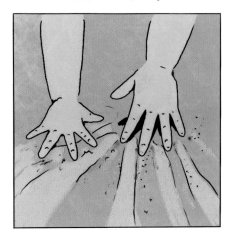

and it is also fine to
minimize mess and let
them do that in the
bathtub,

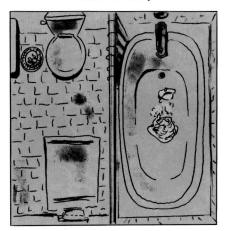

but under no circumstances should you run the water
into the tub before you get the kid out, even if they
think that too would be FUN!

...because water plus flour equals
wheatpaste, and now you have a
miserable crying child with tiny
balls of sticky paste clinging to
every tiny filament of peach
fuzz on their body, and it'll take
days to get it all off.

I've learned that if you do something three days in a row, it's now part of the routine,

☐ Breakfast
☐ Park
☐ Snack
☐ **MUDLARKING**
☐ Lunch

PUMPKIN CATAPULT DAY

12

and if you do it three years in a row, it's a tradition,

so be careful about how many times you seat a stuffed bunny at the kitchen table and serve her a cup of tea.

I've learned that one of the most important things, actually, is that they feel you're on their side. And in my desire to be helpful, always, I have again sat down and tried to write what I know in the hopes that I can have made these mistakes so you don't have to and so you don't feel so alone in the incredible mountain of decision making that parenting requires, so if nothing else it feels... doable.

You can do it. Pinky swear.

Maybe some of what follows will help. Take what you can use, laugh at the rest, and good luck.

A few things
as we get started.

1. If you don't have kids yet, this book may seem pessimistic, but I don't intend it to be.

If you're in the pre-child time, you might read this book and think

The truth is that while parenting could be described that way, it is also

The truth is, I assume you can manage those moments without my assistance and don't need me to tell you things like

REVEL IN THE SWEET MOMENTS!

An advice book is necessarily a bunch of things about which people have asked for my advice, or about which I would have enjoyed better advice than I got, and we need advice about problems, so... that's a lot of what's in here. Please don't be discouraged; instead, think of it as

AN EXPRESSION OF MY CONFIDENCE IN YOUR OVERALL COMMON SENSE..

2. Not everything in this book will apply to you.

In doing research on parenting books, both when I was preparing to parent and when I was preparing to write this book, I noticed that some experiences I think of as being reasonably common in my communities—

—were siloed completely into their own books, and I... do not love this vibe. It makes me feel like some of the ways kids show up in the world are somehow beyond the scope of the "regular" and therefore have to be treated like a Very Special Episode all the time.

While I agree that specifics and complexity and nuance are valuable, I also always want people to feel like their experiences and needs are part of the world, not somehow separate from it.

So as you read, whatever your parenting experience might be, some of what you read may not apply to your experience or your family—yet or ever.

I'm trusting that you're clever enough to know which is which, while also believing strongly that knowing even a little about parenting experiences you don't have (especially if yours are pretty mainstream and already well supported by the larger culture) can only help you and your children in the long run. They will eventually go to school or otherwise join the larger world and become friends with each other,

and when those kids' gardens

look notably different from yours, this is also useful.

3. I will definitely have missed things.

Two things are equally true about this book:

1) I reached out widely to my network of people doing parenting work, and to the children I know, to understand what I might be missing in the ways I write about parenting and frame parenting experiences.

2) I am just one guy.

Definitely I have missed things, and certainly I have had to make choices about what I think is most helpful based on what's already been written about in ways I like, and what I have not seen discussed in the ways I most value. You may well find yourself reading along and notice where I could have said <u>more</u>, included a (larger) diversity of experiences, or treated a topic that is very important to you *more extensively* (or *differently*, or *better*).

There are errors of commission and errors of omission here, even after accepting all the beautiful and necessary work of editing and beta-reading people have generously offered me, and I have had to accept that fact in order to get out of my own way and finish this book. Never has the postcard over my desk that reads

"THE PERFECT IS THE ENEMY OF THE GOOD." —VOLTAIRE

been so frequently consulted and argued with as while I wrote this time.

IS IT?

4. It's never too late to add something you feel is an upgrade.

You'll note as you read that I will sometimes encourage you to plan, consider, and prepare for something before a kid arrives, if possible (however that kid may arrive to your household, at whatever age).

That's optimal if you can manage it, but for so many reasons, your experience may not have happened that way.

The good thing is, it's never too late to try a new thing. That's true even if the ideal window has passed,

even if it has become a source of conflict or difficulty,

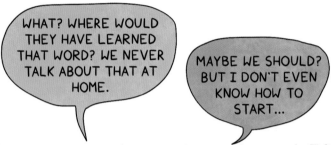

even if your circumstances have changed. If you read something and think,

then do it. Bear in mind, of course, that it can be challenging to create new habits or structures or patterns or programs and even more challenging to stick with them, but try it anyway, even if it feels clunky, awkward, or rocky at the beginning.

7:00AM — Make lunch

7:10AM — Make breakfast

7:20AM — THE NEWS

And, as I am so fond of reminding myself and other people, sometimes naming that awkwardness helps to mitigate the impact of it. If you just say,

WE ARE GOING TO TRY A NEW PRACTICE FOR THE NEXT MONTH AND SEE HOW WE FEEL ABOUT IT

and then play the news at breakfast instead of Disco Hits of the 80s,

it helps. Validating people's feelings around change doesn't preclude going ahead and making change anyway.

⑤ Every kid is different.

I really, really did not understand this part. Like, at all. Somehow I understood that all adults are different, and that different things

motivate   or concern   or cheer

different people, but I did not grasp how very soon that begins.

Even in the very earliest days of infancy, every kid is different, and parenting is always to some degree a process of try, fail, try again. What soothes your first sleepless baby may not soothe the next one.

One might love being swaddled or sung to,

and the next one might act like they've been dipped in acid if you try.

What helped two children feel better after they got their feelings hurt

may fall flat for kiddo number three.

Your strong value about children eating what they want of the one meal you make might be great

until a kid with sensory issues comes along and disrupts your carefully made plans.

Your niecephew might be bold and fully ready to fly alone at age six,

and your kid might be absolutely terrified and unready to even consider it until twelve.

There is a tremendous amount of variation in how children are, what their strengths are, what capacity they have for certain things, what interests them, what repels them. So of course you will first try the thing that worked before—

from an earlier kid,

from babysitting when you were twelve,

from minding your niecephews while your sister and brother-in-law took a weekend away—

but sometimes it won't work on a different kid,

or even on the same kid at a different stage.

This is exhausting but unavoidable.

6. You can't prepare for everything, so you kind of have to prepare for anything.

There's no way to anticipate everything to come, parenting-wise. The absolute weirdest shit crops up, like

one day your child goes to preschool with some sea glass in their pocket

and then loses it

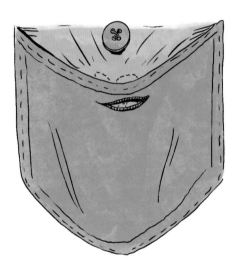

and is inconsolable all day

and receives comfort

but is also firmly told not to bring things they cannot bear to lose, and then the next day and for months afterward they simply refuse to wear anything with pockets and melt into screaming hysterics if you try to put them in their regular shorts because somehow in all of this they have concluded that

POCKETS!

are the root of their unhappiness.

Does this make any sense to an adult brain?

No.

Could you hit them or scream at them until they're
more afraid of you than they are of pockets?

You could, and people do, but you absolutely should not, for two reasons:

1) I don't think violence is a good parenting choice, because it teaches your children you're not a safe person to be near,

and 2) it stops working when they're older, and then you won't have built up any of the trust or cooperation you'll need when bigger problems arise.

So is this just your life now? Separating out all the pants with pockets and trading them on your local Buy Nothing group for some leggings or pocketless sweatpants in the same size?

Yup.

Like a butler or a stage manager or a Navy SEAL, some of the best preparation for parenting is less about practising specific skills and more about practising how to improvise, adapt, and overcome.

The more you can expand your own capacity for flexibility and creativity, the better off you'll be.

Use anything you find in this book as a jumping-off point, a frame, a concept, an idea from which you innovate your own better, more-appropriate-to-your-needs-right-now idea.

You definitely will not love every minute of it, but overall, my bet is? You're going to do just fine.

RECIPE FOR JOY:

- One infant
- One adult
- One couch
- One sunny afternoon

Fold together very gently.

Yield: one delicious nap.

Are we ready to have
a child?

When people casually ask me for parenting advice or support, a few questions come up over and over. The most common one by a considerable margin is

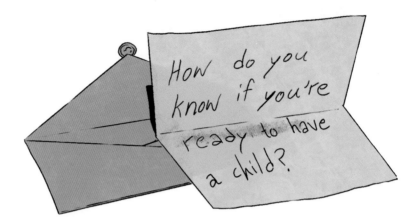

Maybe this is also your question. So let's discuss.

This is an answer that comes in two parts. The first part applies to basically everyone who is considering bringing home a first child, in whatever way, and that answer is:

Don't be discouraged! That doesn't mean you should stop reading, and it doesn't mean you shouldn't have a child. It just means no, you're not ready.

The truth is, and I believe this to the bottom of my soul:

We try to get ready, and sometimes we think we're ready,

but you'll never be ready for how consuming and complicated and life changing it is to be a parent,

or for how a child opens up entire new rooms of love in your heart—

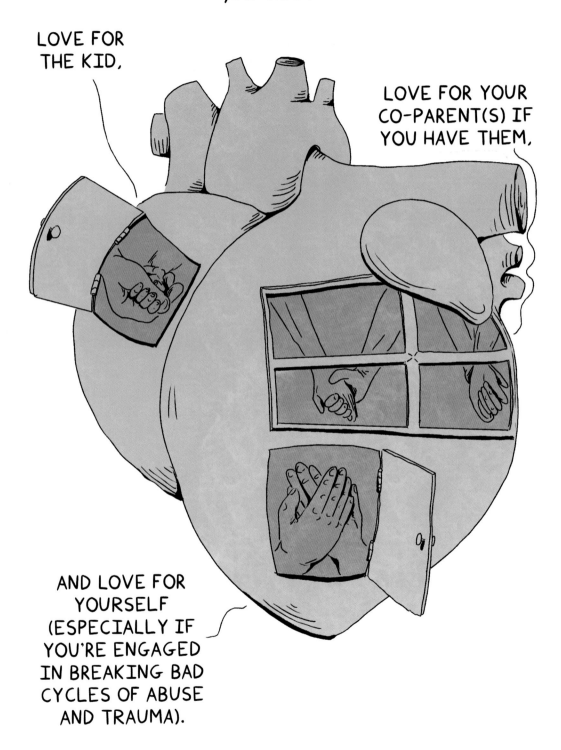

LOVE FOR THE KID,

LOVE FOR YOUR CO-PARENT(S) IF YOU HAVE THEM,

AND LOVE FOR YOURSELF (ESPECIALLY IF YOU'RE ENGAGED IN BREAKING BAD CYCLES OF ABUSE AND TRAUMA).

No one could ever be ready.

The good news is, that's fine.
You're not ready now, and you won't be ready the day you
bring that child home either,

but then you will have an entirely new person who is
simultaneously a critical part of your family and
a total stranger,

and they will eat your whole life and your entire brain,

and the fact that you're not ready will become
considerably less pressing to you because you'll be doing it.
You still won't feel ready, but it's not going to keep you up
nights because now there's this small person who keeps
you up nights instead.

(Please note that this appears to be true at whatever age
your child joins your family, and by whatever means or
method they come to join you. You might think I mean
this only to apply to infants, but I assure you,
I mean all of them.)

But beyond that, I hear you asking,

HOW DO WE <u>KNOW</u> IF WE'RE READY? WHAT ARE THE STEPS, CAPTAIN STEP-BY-STEP? WHERE IS THE CHECKLIST?

1. You've dealt with any hard feelings, issues, or trauma about how you were parented.

The first thing on a lot of people's lists is money. Are we financially stable enough to raise a child? Maybe after one more degree, promotion, or raise we'll be ready;

maybe once we've bought a house, we'll be ready?

Certainly, money is helpful in parenting—you want to be able to feed them and clothe them and keep them warm,

pay for their medications and rain boots and field trips,

take them to minigolf or for an ice cream cone sometimes.

Being broke while parenting is exhausting, and having to perform an ongoing calculus of what you can do without this month wears away at anyone's patience and good humour.

You can also use money to buy back some time,

whether that's getting occasional takeout when you simply cannot manage cooking

or hiring someone to scrub the floors once a month

or whatever arrangement you need to keep this small person safe while you work or maybe even eventually do something fun.

Money helps with all of that, absolutely. But still, it's not the most important thing.

Some of us had great parenting. Certainly there were moments of difficulty, challenges or abruptions, but for some people, using their own parent(s) as a role model for parenting is a great choice.

For others, however... not so much.
We may know that we don't want to parent the way ours did, and we think we are managing most of the big ways the

ABUSE	OR TRAUMA	OR NEGLECT	OR JUST PLAIN POOR CHOICES
◖	◖	◖	◖

of our parents show up in our lives, but friend, let me tell you: in my experience, absolutely nothing brings up bad old patterns and programming like becoming a parent yourself.

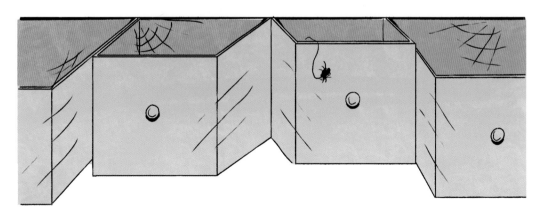

You're sleep deprived,

things are complicated and new,

somehow everyone else seems to be having a truly beautiful time of it

(thank you, social media),

and there you are, just trying to give a toddler some breakfast. You make them a cute plate with a little yogurt and some pureed fruit and maybe little toast batons with cream cheese or peanut butter, possibly before you've even had your own coffee—

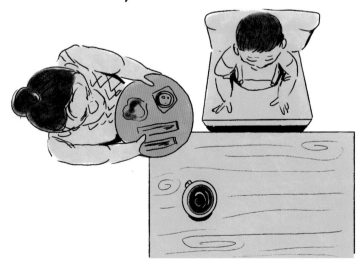

and then they look you right in the eyes,

knock the whole thing onto the floor,

and laugh like this is hilarious.

Do they mean to be horrible? Of course not, they're just experimenting with cause and effect. But it can set off little chain-reaction explosions in your feelings-place when they hit your hot spots (one of mine, clearly, is feeling disrespected).

So it's critical to figure out what your hot spots are

BEEP!

and to do two things about them:

1) Talk them out very thoroughly, either with a paid professional or with close and trusted friends and family who can help you make sense of your deepest feelings,

and 2) Spend extra time thinking about (and discussing with any co-parents, or with close friends if you'll be solo parenting) how you can support one another when you're about to completely lose it (or have just lost it).

Do the work now.

❷ Your relationship(s) with your co-parent(s), if any, are in a good state.

There's a long-time saying among polyamorous folks to describe a very common poor choice people make:

> RELATIONSHIP BROKEN?
> ADD MORE PEOPLE.

It describes the phenomenon in which people find themselves in a relationship moment where they feel like they don't have a shared purpose or their communication has stalled,

so they solve this problem by... getting involved with someone new.

This often works in the short term, because novelty is exciting and hormones are too, and for a while—especially in the anticipatory phases—there's a lot of enthusiasm and generosity and shopping for new cute stuff.

But if the original relationship isn't well connected, communicative, and rooted in shared values, everything goes to hell pretty fast.

So let's try not to create that situation with kids if we can avoid it.

Sometimes I hear this advice:

Get a plant. If the plant is alive in a year, get a dog.

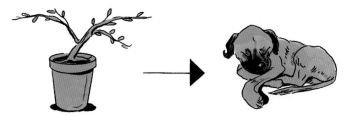

If the dog is alive after a year,
you're ready to have a baby.

I don't hate this advice, but I think it's too specific. What
you really want in order to see if your relationship is ready
for a baby is a shared project. Start small

LET'S HAVE A YARD SALE!

and see how you feel about the process of figuring out who
will do what, what the standard of "good enough" is, and
whether you can achieve it.

How do your partner(s)
respond to critique, and how
much do they critique you?

YOU'RE RIGHT, THE
HANGERS MAKE MORE
SENSE THAN FOLDING!

Do they finish the
parts they're
responsible for?

I THOUGHT YOU
WERE GOING TO
HANG THE SIGNS.

Do they make gendered
assumptions about who
will do which parts?

CAN YOU COME
SORT THROUGH
THE CLOTHES?

How do you feel about all of these things?
If good, level up to a more complex project.

Re-tiling the upstairs bathroom or throwing a fundraiser together will teach you some more things. (One thing it may teach you is that you need a detour back to step one.)

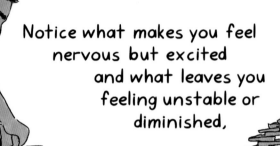

Notice what makes you feel nervous but excited and what leaves you feeling unstable or diminished,

and notice it without much judgment if you can—you are entitled to your own feelings, and they don't have to work like anyone says they should.

If you feel like you and your prospective co-parent(s) are able to hand tasks back and forth with some flow,

CAN YOU PASS THE SPONGE?

FOR SURE, TRADE YOU FOR THE GROUT?

make each other laugh when you're in the shit,

ARE YOU BUILDING A TOWER?

I AM AN ARCHITECT, I HAVE DECIDED.

give and accept critique without it being the End of the World,

ARCHITECT, CAN YOU PAUSE CONSTRUCTION?

YES, SORRY, HERE IS THE SPONGE.

and still like each other when it's over? That's great news.

❸ Someone should be very enthusiastic.

My husband and I have noticed over the years (sixteen and counting) that the only condition under which things get done in a satisfying way in our family is when one of us is very enthusiastic about doing that thing. The other can be merely willing, that's fine; every undertaking does not require double-barrelled enthusiasm to thrive, though that can be very nice. But when he's enthusiastic, I can hitch my rope to his joy or excitement or satisfaction and find my way into it, and vice versa.

When both of us feel... fine about something, willing to do it but not excited, it's very unlikely to happen in the absence of some external factor that requires it.

But no one requires you to have a child, not even if there's family pressure or other kinds of expectation. So really, now is the time for a gut check:

are you excited and enthusiastic about parenting,  or does it just feel like something you're supposed to do?

If it's the former, great.

If no one is actually brimming with excitement, though?
You absolutely can do just a little.

Make a weekly date for tea and books with your favourite
eight-year-old.

Donate money to your local
shelter for at-risk parents
with children.

Give everyone you like who gets pregnant the gift of a
thorough scrub of their bathroom toward the end of the
pregnancy when they're too sick and/or exhausted to do it
themselves. Regardless of whether anyone has been
pregnant, you can also do one when the new kid has been
there about four weeks.

Let the teenagers in your life know
that if they need to be picked up from
somewhere, for any reason, they can
call you for a safe ride at any hour.

These are superlative things you can do to support the wellness of young people without committing yourself to full-time parenting if you're just not that into it.

Bonus: both the parents and the children will deeply value these opportunities, and they contribute to the rich garden of a child's life without you having to be in the rows weeding and watering every single day.

Now, is money nice in parenting?

Absolutely.

Is it easier with your own washer and dryer in your unit or house?

YUP.

Can good insurance get you better services for a child who needs them?

Absolutely.

I'm not saying to ignore the question of money and stability.

What I'm saying is, a lot of excellent parenting happens in households with little money, and a lot of atrocious parenting happens in households with piles of it.

If you're waiting until you're both employed

or until you have enough money for reliable transportation

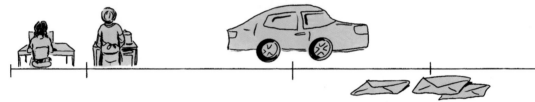

and to pay all of your bills every month, that makes good sense.

(And it can be a heavy lift!)

But after that, if you're focusing on money as the measure of being ready, I would like to gently suggest that there are other issues you might need to attend to at least as urgently.

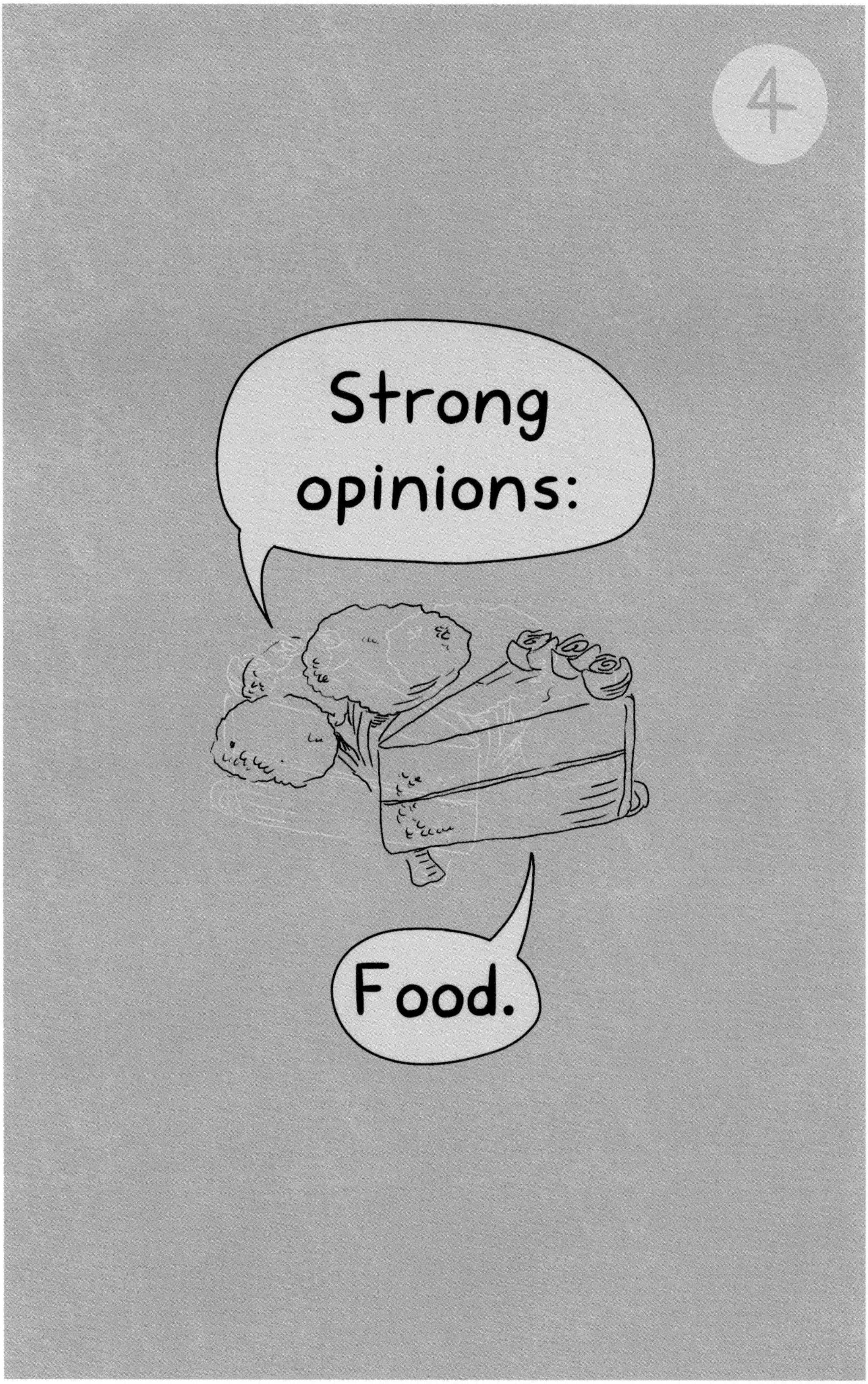
4
Strong opinions:
Food.

Accustom your children early to the idea that cut fruit and/or vegetables, cheese, and crackers are a meal. Add nuts or dips if you feel fancy, but this kind of a quick lunch/dinner is good for so many moments.

A great way to make new foods exciting rather than intimidating is to start with snacks and candy.

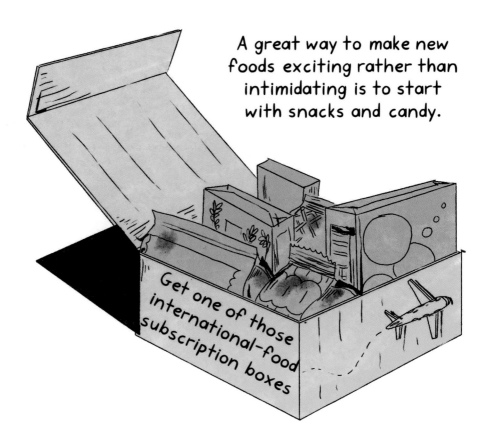

Get one of those international-food subscription boxes

or take field trips to the international markets nearby

and let them pick chocolates or chips or pop that look interesting,

then take them home to taste test and discuss.

CRUNCHIER THAN PRETZELS!

UNEXPECTEDLY STRONG CRAB FLAVOUR?

It's an easily transferable enthusiasm if you encourage (but don't require) kids to taste new things (or to try again if it has been a few years).

Adding in new cheeses and new fruits after new candy and snacks is a nice step.

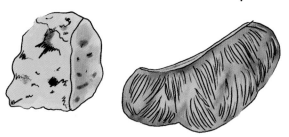

I like Ellyn Satter's idea that there should be a division of labour at the table:

the adults provide the food, which is our part of the work,

and the children eat what and how much they want, which is their part.

I also think about this in terms of hospitality—if you want children to feel welcome at the table and pleased about food, cook for them like they're guests.

Don't comment on how much they eat or which things— though when they're small you can remind a distractable child that it's also eating time and not just talking time.

...CAME THE CAT AND ATE THE GOAT THAT MY FATHER BOUGHT FOR TWO ZUZIM...

Be glad that they're there and that you're eating together.

Food aversions are real, and some kids simply can't stand certain tastes or textures of food.

In this way too, treat them like guests—make sure there are at least some foods on the table that they feel comfortable with, and don't try to browbeat them into eating things they feel dubious about. Keep thinking about hospitality.

 If fresh fruit is too texturally uncertain, offer frozen or freeze dried; maybe that's nicer.

 If most cheese is too smelly or strong, keep halloumi or queso fresco on hand.

They won't starve, I promise—and the paradox here is that people who feel complete agency to not eat anything they do not want are more likely to go ahead and choose to try something when they feel ready to experiment.

Relevant to the above, there are a million versions of "make-your-own-sundaes," all great for feeding children: rice bowls, tacos, ramen, pizza, sushi rolls, nachos.

Basically, make or buy the base,

prep a bunch of vegetables (and fish or eggs or meat or tofu) to go with the starch of choice,

set out sauces as desired,

and let everyone roll their own, if you will. They can experiment as much or as little as they want, and you can skip complaints and short-order cooking.

One person can just eat the plain chicken chunks with rice (or the equivalent)

while someone else mixes four different textures of food and drowns it in sauce,

and yet everyone is eating the same meal.

Great snacks you may not have thought of:

SNAP PEAS WITH BLUE CHEESE DRESSING

POPCORN WITH BUTTER AND NUTRITIONAL YEAST

TOAST WITH CREAM CHEESE AND JAM

No fat shaming, ever.

No diet talk or, Gd forbid, dieting, ever.

It's not good for anyone, but it's really not good for children.

Nobody needs to earn their food,

no one is being naughty when they eat doughnuts,

no one is being good when they eat an apple.

Broccoli is delicious, and so is cake.

Your thighs are fine, and so are theirs.

5

It's not the same for everyone: a letter.

Friends, Saul and I have decided that I will write you a letter about this topic (and a few others) instead of having a fully illustrated chapter.
This is for two reasons:

1) neither of us wants to create images of kids and families being miserable or treated badly, because that feels awful, and

2) the chapters about the hardest stuff necessarily include a lot of oppressive behaviours, so we would be making images that disproportionately showed kids and families from equity-seeking groups being miserable or treated badly, which feels even worse.

When you see these letter-chapters, please know that they will be very lightly illustrated and that we have chosen this out of love and care.

Dear Brave Correspondent,

As a parent I am constantly crashing into the ways that systems and forms and institutions do not expect my family, from all the many, many times I have been asked

WHERE'S THE MOTHER?

(usually with benign intention) to the recently more common suspicion that I, as a queer dad, have acquired children in order to abuse them. This comes up when forms ask for a

_____
MOTHER'S MAIDEN NAME

and it comes up when a camp counsellor says,

ASK YOUR MOTHER TO PACK YOU MORE SNACK TOMORROW

and on and on. We have been lucky to have the agency and the networks and the educational privilege and the whiteness and the money and the time to select schools and camps and programs that will welcome a queer family, or at least tolerate us without a lot of nonsense. But every choice comes with the requirement to check ahead and often to do education ahead to make sure as best we can that our kids have a safe experience, which is a lot of work. So I thought I really understood this.

Then, I was having a conversation on a Facebook parenting group about Pyjama Day at preschool. A mom posted that her kiddo wanted to keep wearing pyjamas to school, and the general consensus was

> EH, THEY'RE FOUR YEARS OLD, WHY NOT?

and I cheerfully agreed. Why not? Wear your fire truck pyjamas all week, who cares; I can wash them overnight if I have to. But then, a disabled mom posted to say:

> JUST A COUNTERPOINT HERE: I WANT TO ALLOW THIS BUT I DON'T FEEL SAFE DOING IT BECAUSE I'M AFRAID SOMEONE WOULD CALL CHILD PROTECTIVE SERVICES AND REPORT THAT WE CAN'T PROPERLY DRESS OR CARE FOR OUR CHILD.

When she was challenged,

> REALLY? I CAN'T IMAGINE THAT HAPPENING.

other disabled parents chimed in to report that they had been summoned to concerned meetings with teachers or had calls or visits from CPS when their children went on hair-brushing strikes and looked a little messy, when their kids had worn pyjamas or Halloween costumes to school, and even when their kids were slow to learn how to use the toilet paper thoroughly enough because they have a bidet at home.

Just a little while after that, a Twitter conversation erupted about... apple picking. Specifically, the wholesome autumnal activity of taking your children to eat sun-warmed apples and wear themselves out running around a nearby orchard.
Black Twitter asked:

> When you were a child, if you were taken to a U-Pick situation, were you allowed to eat any apples or other fruit before you paid?

Uniformly, Black adults said they were not, nor did they allow their children to, for fear of being accused of stealing fruit. Again, people not affected by the systemic problem (in this case, non-Black people) challenged this concern—oh no, they said, every orchard I have ever been to allows this. They expect that you'll eat a few while you pick. And again, people who were affected by it said

> IN FACT, I HAVE BEEN THE TARGET OF THIS KIND OF SCRUTINY AT AN APPLE ORCHARD OR IN A STRAWBERRY PATCH.

When I started listening for examples, they cropped up aplenty. White people who were pregnant reported that their doctors said a glass of wine every now and then was fine and not to stress about it, while Indigenous people had their babies taken away at birth because they reported occasionally drinking a beer while pregnant.

Single moms got condescending little lectures from their sons' baseball coaches about the importance of a man in the house to play catch with the boys, while married moms whose husbands were never seen or heard from during baseball practice did not.

Jewish parents (including us) received dire warnings about hampering our children's academic progress by keeping them out of school during Jewish holidays, but Christian parents who took their kids out of school early for break so they could travel to see family were warmly wished a festive holiday season. White parents felt safe telling their children to find a police officer to ask for help if they somehow got separated, but Black and brown parents told their children that if they got separated, they should find someone else with children.

I could do an entire book of this bullshit if I wanted to before we even touched the ways systems are not set up to welcome and celebrate GIaNT (gender-independent, non-binary, trans) kids or disabled kids or kids with learning disabilities/differences/challenges or kids who have complex medical needs or severe food allergies or whatever other exceptionalities put them beyond what an institution expects.

You may now be asking

WHY ARE YOU TELLING ME THIS?

 If you're a parent (or parent-to-be) from an equity-seeking group or with a kid who is, you already know. If you're not, then why do you need to worry about other people's experiences?

The truth is, I find seeking to understand what contexts other people are operating within an important value. It helps me make more equitable choices, and it prepares me to do allyship work. Also, there's always more to learn about other people's experiences. This chapter is largely intended to serve as a reminder that even if you are a parent who is never required to think about these issues, you don't have to remain unaffected by them.

You can advocate for more inclusive policies just as vigorously as you would if it were your kid (and, exhaustingly, you're more likely to be listened to if your family isn't affected by a policy than if you are, because you are perceived as a neutral party, so take a list of talking points from the people who would be affected and then go champion policies that support them). You can remind and reinforce for your children that minor, common childhood transgressions like playing ding-dong-ditch or climbing the school building after hours or shoplifting a pack of gum or sneaking a beer out of the fridge to drink in the park may have different consequences for different kids, even though they've all committed the same infraction.

You can make sure your house is a place where kids, and their families, are not just generally welcome but specifically welcomed, by trying to imagine what concerns they might have and planning to address them before someone has to figure out whether they have the strength to ask about them and then explain them and then make their own mitigation plan.

But mostly, honestly? I want you to think about it, friend. I want you to hold on to the critical fact that parenting may be the same job for everyone, but it's not the same work for everyone. If you experience that additional amount of work, maybe holding this knowledge will help you extend yourself some grace for the good job you're doing in difficult circumstances, and if you experience less work, maybe it will spur you to give yourself an assignment that relieves a bit of someone else's undue burden.

I think remembering that it's not the same for everyone makes us all better parents—better for our kids, and better for the world.

love and courage,

Bear

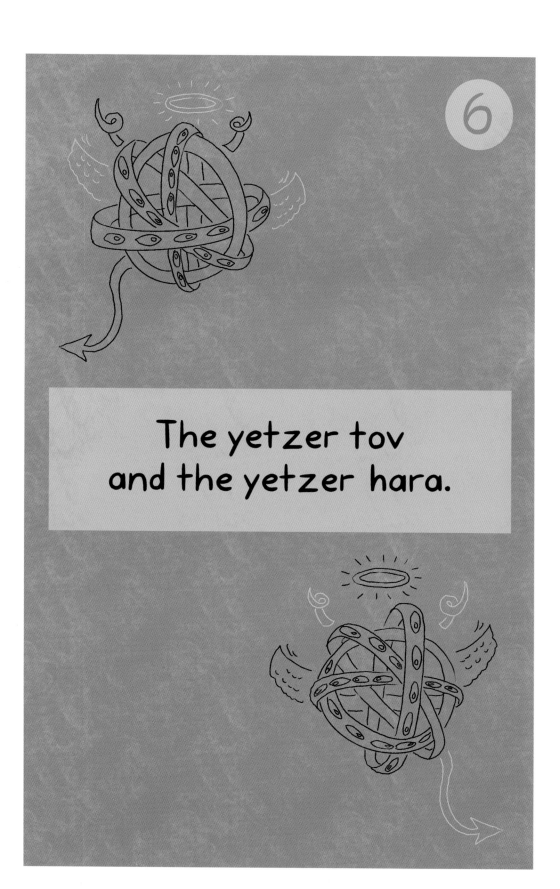

The yetzer tov
and the yetzer hara.

In Judaism there's a concept that every person has within them, at all times, two different voices speaking to them:

the yetzer tov, or the good inclination,

and the yetzer hara, or the bad inclination.

It's a common concept

(see also: an angel on one shoulder and a devil on the other),

and many cultures contain it, but in Judaism I think it has particular resonance, because in most cases it is not considered bad, necessarily, to have the urge to do a bad thing, if one doesn't act on it.

This is a framing I find critical in parenting: wanting to do a bad thing doesn't make you bad,

and neither does wanting to do a good thing make you good.

It's our behaviour that matters, more than our impulses (or even our intentions).

Because, of course, it's tempting to do things we know we shouldn't,

whether that's sneaking extra candy

or lying to stay out of trouble

or kicking someone who is acting like a real jerk,

and I don't think there's a lot of value in shaming a kid (or an adult) for having the idea to do it.

Instead, I appreciate the framing of the yetzer tov and the yetzer hara. Of course the bad thing occurs to you.

Of course you might want to skip school

or want to get your iPad in the middle of the night when you know you're not supposed to have it

or want to say something unkind when you feel upset.

That doesn't make you a bad person; that's just the yetzer hara talking, as it always does.

The process of growing into a thoughtful and trustworthy person isn't about never having the urge to do something that you know is wrong but would feel good in the moment; it's about growing and strengthening the discernment to ignore the yetzer hara and listen to the yetzer tov, the voice that says

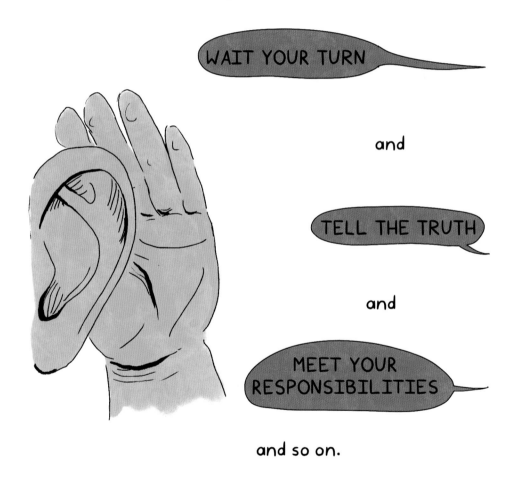

WAIT YOUR TURN

and

TELL THE TRUTH

and

MEET YOUR RESPONSIBILITIES

and so on.

I know there are religious and cultural traditions that contain the idea of

SINNING IN ONE'S HEART,

the notion that wanting to do the bad thing is just as bad as doing it. My fear about this, on a parenting level, is that it focuses kids away from choosing a correct and just action because they already feel sunk.

If they've already transgressed by considering sneaking an extra cookie,

then why not actually take the cookie

and then lie if they're asked about it,

I WOULD NEVER!

because after all, they're already bad.

What I value in teaching about the yetzer tov and the yetzer hara is that it focuses kids' attention instead on the actions they take, on how they participate in the world, which feels much more within a person's control.

As a parent, I also find this helpful for myself. As a notably impatient person who struggles constantly with the impulse to yell about things, I have really worried about how this would affect my kids. I never want to be impatient with them.

I sometimes am anyway, but I have learned that this is a place where I need to really, really tune in to my own yetzer tov and take the better action, even when my yetzer hara is practically shouting at me.

Turns out, I haven't become any more patient since I've had children (less, probably, because I'm not sleeping as much and someone is always interrupting me).

However, I have considerably developed my ability to imagine what a patient person would do and to do that,

because it turns out that what I actually do matters a lot more than what I first consider doing, and I am also more able to turn down the self-flagellating inner voice telling me I'm an awful parent because my first impulse isn't my best one—

both abilities that are pretty much exactly what I want for my children as well.

RECIPE FOR JOY:

- One hobby or interest
- One set of supplies for that hobby or interest
- Children to taste

Mix regularly.

Yield: days of companionably pursuing that hobby together, sharing tips and ideas.

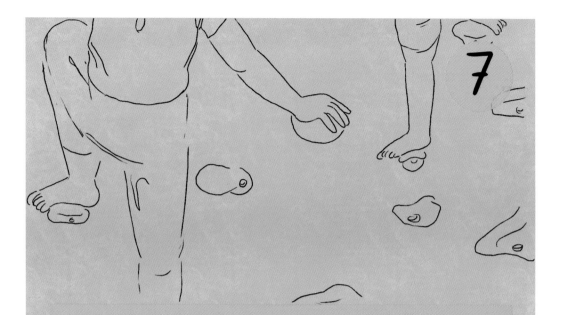

Six useful things
I say all the time.

1. Look out for everyone littler than you.

2. Make your case.

3. Use your resourcefulness and figure it out.

4. This is the last time I'm going to be able to ask you calmly.

5. If you can get up there, you can be up there.

6. On a scale of one to ten, how important is this?

①. Look out for everyone littler than you.

This started in that incredibly exciting (and alarming!) location of children's joy into which adults typically cannot accompany them: the bounce house.

I did not understand until my tiny human badly wanted to enter one, and I peered in and saw children of all sizes careening around in the dim interior, crashing into each other, the bigger kids heedlessly causing the littlest ones to literally fly through the air just by bouncing near them.

Terrifying. And also so much fun.

So, as has been my habit—as a worrywart with adventure-model children—I took a deep breath and let them go. Before they went in, though, I said

LOOK OUT FOR EVERYONE LITTLER THAN YOU.

At that age, there weren't a lot of beings littler than that kid; to be honest, I said it mostly hoping the bigger kids already flinging themselves headlong into the walls would also hear me and take heed.

But soon, it became a ritual. Whenever I would release them into a bounce house or onto the playground or at the skating rink or wherever, I would remind them (in a carrying tone) to look out for everyone littler than them.

And most of the time, they did.

I noticed that when they made up games, even the youngest kids could play,

and that they went out of their way to encourage kids who looked hesitant to join in,

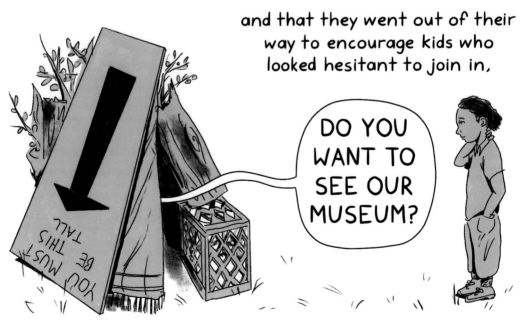

and that they'd check on kids who'd fallen down or gotten a bump to make sure they weren't injured.

I'll never forget a day at the rock wall of a playground we were visiting, when a smaller kid climbed high and got too scared to descend.

One of my children scrambled up, quick as anything, and very patiently talked that kid down,

foothold by foothold,

eye to eye,

encouraging them the entire way,

while I tried to pretend I was not crying.

(Eventually we were able to extrapolate the idea that being bigger or stronger also comes with responsibilities more broadly, and we continued on to using it as a base for talking about privilege and power, but honestly it's useful however much you embellish.)

② Make your case.

When I went to university, I attended Hampshire College. Instead of a traditional situation where a student has a major and takes a series of classes as directed, Hampshire had a portfolio system. At each of three stages,

students had to write a proposal for the work they wanted to do to meet the broad requirements of that "level,"

then find a faculty member (or, in the third and final stage, a committee) to agree to evaluate the work.

Though I learned a lot at university, both in classes and during my various projects, the skill I practised there that has served me the most in post-college life was crafting a proposal and making my argument to the faculty advisors I wanted.

Because of this, I'm a great fan of asking a child to make their case.

I like watching them rise to the challenge, and I love to see a serious little face marshalling an argument,

even if sometimes in the morning I would like less argument and more putting on your shoes, please.

I want them to develop the skills of planning and preparing to get someone engaged in their need or desire

and also of accepting a no with some grace and good humour.

WIGGLE AT HOME, PLEASE!

This has the added benefit of not just giving kids confidence in their skills, but also increasing their total ratio, if you will; it's easy to feel defeated and like a failure if you make one ask

MAY I GO TO SCHOOL BAREFOOT?

and get one no.

YOU MAY NOT.

But if a kid enters life beyond the purview of their parents with a track record—

some yeses,

MAY I WEAR MY SPARKLY SHOES?

OF COURSE!

some nos,

MAY I WEAR THEM IN GYM CLASS?

NO, THEY DO NOT HAVE ENOUGH TREAD.

and some ask-again-laters

MAY I STOP HAVING GYM CLASS?

WHEN YOU ARE IN HIGH SCHOOL.

—their early failures might not feel so devastating while they recalibrate to new situations, because they have grown some confidence in advocating for themselves.

3. Use your resourcefulness and figure it out.

This one is a mixed bag, like many things of parenting. I say it often because I want to raise sturdy problem solvers who don't crumple at the first moment of complication or adversity, but be advised: they will learn to figure things out, and sometimes the solutions will not be what you would have suggested. They will be short-sighted

or dangerous

or so singular in focus that everything in their way is simply an obstacle to clear, regardless of any knock-on effects (which they are too little to predict for some years).

Here's the thing, though: let them do the thing imperfectly or messily sometimes. Let them have the satisfaction of doing it themselves.

Also, not for nothing, the more things they can figure out how to do for themselves, the fewer times they will need to interrupt you to get a bowl or to supervise how much yogurt they put in it.

4. This is the last time I'm going to be able to ask you calmly.

I just find this one useful as a warning that I am reaching the end of my patience and that the time for farting around has passed. Sometimes I notice that my children don't pay a lot of attention to my requests until I yell about them,

and I am constantly trying to reduce or eliminate the amount of yelling I do, so this is my compromise position: I alert them that

YELLING IS NOW ON THE HORIZON,

and they would be well advised to listen before the yelling starts if, as they say, they want less yelling.

If you're not inclined to yelling, this one may be less useful to you, but I find it invaluable to have in my pocket, especially on days when I am barely keeping it together as it is and I need more cooperation, sooner than usual.

5. If you can get up there, you can be up there.

My children used to constantly ask me to put them up on things: playground equipment, trees, rocks, walls, sculptures and statuary, you name it.

But what I noticed was that once they were up there, they would freeze—they lacked the confidence to operate because once they were actually up, it felt too high.

These were the most likely times they would freak out or fall off things, which ruined many outings. Eventually, I crystallized my position as

IF YOU CAN GET UP THERE, YOU CAN BE UP THERE

which certainly caused some short-term wailing from time to time, but learning to do dangerous things carefully is an important part of child development, and I have found that in the long run, it has caused them to be both more competent and more confident,

even if I sometimes discover them so high up it makes my belly flip over unpleasantly and I have to take several deep breaths in order to not freak out (also an important parenting skill).

It also means there are hardly any screams of

I CAN'T GET DOWN!

from across the playground, which I prefer, both as a reduction of their anxiety and as an improvement on my ability to work or read quietly while they play at the park.

6. On a scale of one to ten, how important is this?

Sometimes my children dearly, deeply want me to do something that's difficult or expensive, and somewhat counterintuitively, I often return the agency around the decision to them by framing it like this:

GOING BACK FOR YOUR STUFFIE RIGHT NOW IS GOING TO COST EIGHT DOLLARS IN PARKING

AND TAKE US FORTY-FIVE MINUTES LONGER TO GET HOME,

SO FOR ME IT'S AN 8 OF DIFFICULTY,

AND I AM ALREADY WORRYING ABOUT GETTING HOME TO COOK DINNER,

AND FYI, DINNER WOULD BE FROZEN RAVIOLI AND JAR SAUCE AT BEST.

IF I GO BACK IN THE MORNING, IT'S A 4 OF DIFFICULTY.

ON A SCALE OF ONE TO TEN, HOW URGENT IS IT THAT YOU HAVE THE PLUSH SEA SLUG BACK TONIGHT?

Sometimes it's a

or a

and then I just have to suck it up and go back. This is part of the compact; if their number is higher than mine, I respect it. (I also do not offer this if I am 100 percent not willing to do what they want.) But I find my kids are quite thoughtful about it—they trust that I will honour their assessment,

and I trust that they won't just rate everything a 10 to get their way, and we don't have to have a fight about it.

8

Instead of a family tree,
make a family garden.

I am not quite completely against family trees, but the truth is, I've never been a big fan—mostly because they reduce a story to a diagram, and the diagram you're left with isn't even very good. Due to my very diligent great-aunt Flora, I know the names of my third cousins twice removed on my father's father's side, the daughters of the daughters of my great-great-grandfather

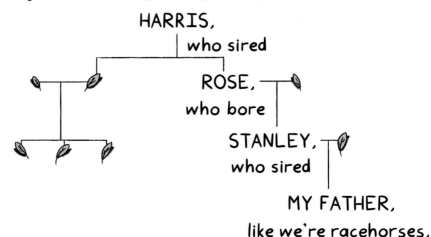

HARRIS,
who sired

ROSE,
who bore

STANLEY,
who sired

MY FATHER,
like we're racehorses,

but I don't and can't and never will know the name of the man who bundled my great-grandfather Harry (who sired Rita, who bore my father) into a cargo berth on a ship bound for America and saved his life, in doing so enabling mine.

I don't know what he risked to do it or if he survived his action or whether he did it for love or money or solidarity with Harry, who had been accused of poisoning horses belonging to the invading Cossacks and had a bounty on his head. I sure would like to though.

Even so, I'm lucky to know that much.

Plenty of people have only smaller fragments after genocides and enslavement,

and more still entered a foster or adoption system that snapped every thread, for better or for worse (usually worse, let's be honest).

When those kids are asked to make or even think about a family tree, what happens? Research shows: nothing good. (Feel free to give "adopted kids + family tree" a quick google if you're skeptical about this.)

So instead, I would like to encourage you to talk with your children about their family garden.

What's better about that?

①. A garden is more flexible.

A kid may have more or fewer than two parents/caregivers,

parents/caregivers they're not related to through genetics or marriage,

important caregivers they are related to but who are not their parents,

or genetically related parents who don't care for them.

They may have aunties, uncles, spuncles, sparkles, bigs, step-parents, vice-parents, step-parents emeritus, godparents, fairy godparents, birth parents, previous parents, donors, diblings, or other people who make up part of their family—

the people who grow with them, and those with whom they grow.

All of those people are important connections in their world. Reducing their family to blood and marriage has the potential both to exclude people a child feels connected to and to include people they're not connected to.

Thinking and talking about a child's family as a garden opens up the construction of family to anyone that child feels close with, and it also allows conversation—which is sometimes needed—about how sometimes plants spontaneously sprout, and it's wonderful...

and sometimes they're not a great fit for that garden, and the boundaries have to be redrawn around them.

You can also discuss what supports a garden,

from sun and rain

to birds and bees and butterflies,

and what things in your environment, small and large, beautiful and grotesque, help a garden to grow.

❷ A garden gives them a broader picture of the world.

Even if you are singly-married heterosexual parents with children who are genetically related to both of you,

I'm sure you know that's not everyone's situation. The sooner your children are able to understand that, the better for everyone. Talking about or making a family garden gives you opportunities to discuss all the ways that children come into the world and all the kinds of families there are.

This does two things: it prepares them to meet kids whose families aren't as straightforwardly linear as yours currently is,

and it populates the landscape of their imagination with many kinds of families in which they may someday wish to participate.

Do you want them to have a flourishing and nourishing family garden as adults?

Of course.

Is it important to you exactly what that garden looks like in the details?

I bet not.

Talking about a family garden now opens up healthy possibilities for them in the near term and also in the further future, where a loving garden—rather than specifically marriage and children—are the goals.

3. Even if your family garden isn't
a straight row, your kids' origin story
is still easy to represent and discuss.

Rather than try to figure out how or when to tell children
how they came to be part of your family, discuss and draw
it from the beginning so they always know their story.
However they joined your family, here is where you can
celebrate everyone who helped you become an us.

While we're here: if your kids' family garden is more
variegated, it really helps them to be in community with
other kids who have similar stories. (If this kind
of community isn't locally available and finances can
stretch, consider a queer family camp.)

Children normalize their own experience, so they assume
however their household operates is how all households do—
until they begin receiving outside feedback.

What you want here is to make connection with other families who share this part of your experience, and for your kids to see, know, and get support from other kids in similar situations. Sometimes support is being able to say who you arrived with and not have anyone ask any questions,

and sometimes support is just a fellow 7-year-old's hearty "ugh, that sucks" to a story about someone's weird vibes toward their queer fam.

4. A garden naturally knows seasonality.

My kids' family garden includes whole raised beds of people whom they only get to see in person once or twice a year, at best. When we visit them, that part of the garden is in its season of abundance:

they get to go to sleep and wake up with those people, see them daily, go on adventures with them, learn new things together and show what each has learned in the interregnum, eat every meal together, and otherwise bask in a sense of plenty.

But not all of those people are great at being in regular contact via mail or electronic methods, and that can be challenging with small children, even for the most diligent connectors.

HOW IS SCHOOL?

Rather than count out people like this (or people who are beloved but rarely or inconsistently available for any of a number of reasons) because they can't be part of a kid's daily life, talk about them as people who have a short season of abundance and then a long fallow period in your garden, saving up all their energy to bloom and fruit the next time you're all together.

5. A garden accounts for complementarity and incompatibility.

Some flowers and fruits or vegetables grow really well when planted close together, and some aren't very compatible.

You may also have friends or family members who get along swimmingly, even when you're not with them, even if they seem extremely different in temperament or interests.

Others, you may utterly adore but find that they do not adore one another.

A family garden allows you to discuss this openly and to note that not everything (or everyone) you enjoy grows best in the same row or can be eaten in the same dish,

like your brother, the globe-trotting muralist, and your sister, who works in pharmaceutical sales, who can't be together for ten unstructured minutes without arguing. They can both be very fine humans who love your children very much, but perhaps when you draw out your family garden, you give them plenty of space from each other.

Or, perhaps you have relatives who are still in your garden for your own reasons, but, like mint, need to be planted in a pot so they stay put and don't stray into areas where they're not wanted.

Maybe they're very delicate and require a greenhouse and special food and additional precautions, but we still hold them close in our hearts, even if we can't enjoy them too vigorously.

Maybe something else, some other metaphor, is at work, but there are people we may have in our family garden whom we need to plant far away from ourselves for everyone to grow well.

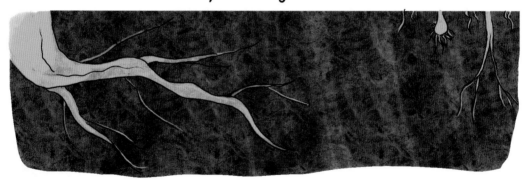

Rather than try to hide strained relationships from your children, honour their perceptions with the truth and reassure them that their garden is their own, and they can grow close beside people from whom you need distance (a concept I had modelled for me as a child regarding my grandmother, who was by all accounts a very difficult mother to have but was an absolutely superlative grandmother and whom I miss daily, still).

BONUS ACTIVITY:

If you might find it helpful or relevant, you can make a garden for your entire family and include all the people and institutions that help you all to grow and bloom.

This can be a lovely way to acknowledge the supports they provide—for complex medical needs, social or emotional support, or other—to help you as a family find your best season.

Very tenderly, I will also say that sometimes, when one member of the family needs a lot of people or structures to bloom their best, this can be a way to take in the whole picture and see where or how other members of the family could benefit from some additional planting to give them more of what they need.

9

On bullying,
harassment,
and violence:
a letter.

Dear Brave Correspondent,

I don't want to be writing to you about this,
but here we are. Sometimes needs must.
Finish your coffee and let's go.

First things first: I hate the word "bullying," and yet
I have no other useful way to describe the kind of
interpersonal emotional or physical violence that
children and teens inflict upon one another. If I say
"school violence," people think I mean school shootings
(also a major concern), and so I have acquiesced for
now to the word "bullying" for this purpose, but I
don't like it. It feels much too small and far too easily
dismissed; it's a very "aw, you know how kids can be"
word. Yes, I do know how kids can be, and that is
why we need better language. But for now, fine.

There are two situations we need to talk about here:

1) your child is being bullied, and

2) your child is bullying others.

Neither is good, but both can be managed, if you're
strongly proactive. Buckle up.

If your child is being bullied at school, the first and most important thing I need you to know is that it is absolutely not their fault, and anyone who suggests the bullying would lessen if your child was different—less weird, less clever, more gender compliant, whatever—is a fool and has no place in education. Unfortunately, there are a lot of these, and even more unfortunately, many of them are former (and unreformed) bullies themselves who went into education so they would always be larger and have more institutional power than almost everyone they see at work all day. You can tell immediately if you are dealing with this kind of a person because they will start victim-blaming immediately upon conclusion of the platitudes portion of the program.

OF COURSE, HERE AT VIOLENT COLONIZER MIDDLE SCHOOL, WE HAVE A ZERO-TOLERANCE POLICY TOWARD ANY ACTS OF BULLYING. BUT I HAVE TO SAY, MR. AND MRS. PATEL, THAT I THINK IT WOULD BE A LOT EASIER FOR GAYATRI IF SHE JUST...

VIOLENT COLONIZER MIDDLE SCHOOL

Bullshit. It will not be easier for Gayatri if she changes how she acts or how she is, because she is not the problem here, and neither is your child. The problem is that shit rolls downhill, and kids who are made to feel shitty about themselves (or as though their acceptability for love is contingent on flawless compliance) will try to reclaim a shred of feeling powerful by making someone else feel like shit, because that is the only method available to a child.

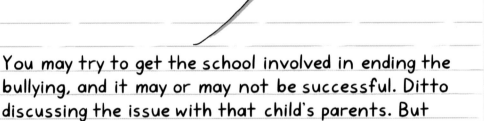

You may try to get the school involved in ending the bullying, and it may or may not be successful. Ditto discussing the issue with that child's parents. But there are things within your control that you can do.

1. Be your child's champion, not their alpha bully.

You may find that, from the depths of your desire for your kid to be okay and your fear for their wellness or safety, your instinct is to try to make them more socially acceptable by pushing them to change their body or behaviour or other kinds of expression.
Do <u>not</u> do this. Let me repeat: do not do this.

I was a nerdy, fat, gender-noncompliant kid whose relatives pushed me to develop more socially acceptable interests, to go on diets, to dress in trendy clothes, and to express a gender more like those of my same-sex classmates. The truth is, while I have generally unpleasant memories of school and a few blistering recollections of specific awful things other children did to me, my memories of the ways I was found unacceptable within my family are much worse and more enduring. It may seem like you're being helpful, as I'm sure it did to my relatives, but not only does it not help, it does harm when the people closest to a child push them to be less true to themselves, and it definitely does not help them to feel safe and loved.

❷ Validate their feelings, even when those feelings are awful and make you want to vomit.

It's really, really hard to hear from a kid that they're being targeted for bullying, and sometimes the first impulse is to try to make it Not True by attempting to recast what's happening in a more friendly light.

MAYBE HE HITS YOU BECAUSE HE LIKES YOU

MAYBE SHE DIDN'T MEAN IT LIKE IT SOUNDED

I'M SURE SHE'S STILL YOUR FRIEND EVEN THOUGH SHE SAID SHE WASN'T ANYMORE

Don't do this. It just teaches your child that they can't trust you with their feelings.

Instead, take time to listen, validate, and, if they want, to strategize, but be aware that strategizing... may not really work. Bullying is so rarely about the kid who is being bullied and almost always entirely about the kid doing the bullying having decided, for some reason and on some day, that they can steal the power they crave from your child. But even when the news is hard, hard, hard, stay in it with them and witness their upset.

3. Do what you need to do to find settings that display them like the gem they are.

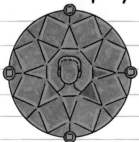

Make sure home and family are safe, supportive, and loving, but also, find places where your kiddo fits in. As much as your resources (time, money, energy) possibly allow, research and facilitate camps, activities, programs, and social gatherings with other kids who share their interests or traits or background.

You want them to have at least some sips of the idea that there's nothing wrong with them, that they can be socially successful and have friends and be valued for their encyclopedic knowledge of Norse myths or their wild outfits or their race or ethnicity or culture or religion or gender or family rather than be mocked because of it.

Depending on the age and temperament of your child, some of these may be kid spaces and some may be largely adult spaces that welcome a junior member, but regardless, keep trying until you find them.
It really helps.

4. Prepare for the possibility that they may have to fight back.

No one wants this, of course. Restorative resolution that takes everyone's humanity and wellness into account is obviously the best outcome in ending a campaign of harassment. (The other kid moving away also works.) But the hard news is that research shows the number one way for a child to get a bully to leave them alone is to hit them, hard.

If a situation has escalated to the point where this starts to feel like the last option left, where it's the bully's safety or your kid's safety, you may need to help your child prepare to do this and make your own preparations for the inevitable phone call you will get about it.

From experience, I can tell you that this is true. After years of antisemitic comments and harassment, like throwing change at me to see if I would pick it up and thus confirm that I was money hungry, like all Jews, I finally snapped my pencil one day and smacked Justin T. right in the mouth in the school cafeteria for saying yet another stupid anti-Jew thing, and he never did it again.

I hate that this is so, and it doesn't make the bully stop bullying entirely. However, done decisively, it will make them leave your child alone and go looking for a different target. This is simultaneously truly awful and sometimes necessary.

Remember, "empowerment" means to give someone power, and we do not, culturally, give very much power to children. So if they feel safe and loved and listened to and reasonably free to fuck up and still be safe and loved, a child's struggles around power are for more agency, more decision making: having ice cream whenever they want or controlling their own bedtime or whether they really have to wear a jacket or attempting to convince you that Hunger Games isn't too scary to watch before bed because they absolutely, definitely, will not be kept awake with nightmares.

But. If a child doesn't feel safe and loved, then they crave the kind of power that makes them feel safe somewhere. If a kid doesn't feel safe at home, then "safe somewhere" very often means making sure other people, somewhere, are afraid of them. If your kid is bullying others, you will definitely need the help of a certified mental health professional and possibly medication, talk therapy, or other interventions (not just me, an advice guy), but a thing I must insist you consider as part of your work is why your child needs to steal power in order to make themselves feel better and who is causing them to feel bad about themselves. You may need to take a very hard look at yourself, your family system, the school environment, the people your child spends time with—especially the adults and older children—and even the media they consume. That may not be the whole answer, but it's pretty likely part of it, and you may need to change your parenting or the people in your kid's life—in concert with restorative work like therapy of various kinds—in order to help them make positive change. Absent significant mental health issues, kids who feel good about themselves don't go around working to make other people feel bad about themselves. If your kid is bullying, your job is to figure out what's happening for them and to do whatever it takes to help them reconnect to their intrinsic goodness and regain a sense of safety. (You may also need external support from friends, professionals, or other community to make it happen.)

Either way, this is such hard stuff, friend. If this chapter is relevant for you, I've been there, and I'm sorry. A million deep breaths and good luck to all of us.

love and courage,

Bear

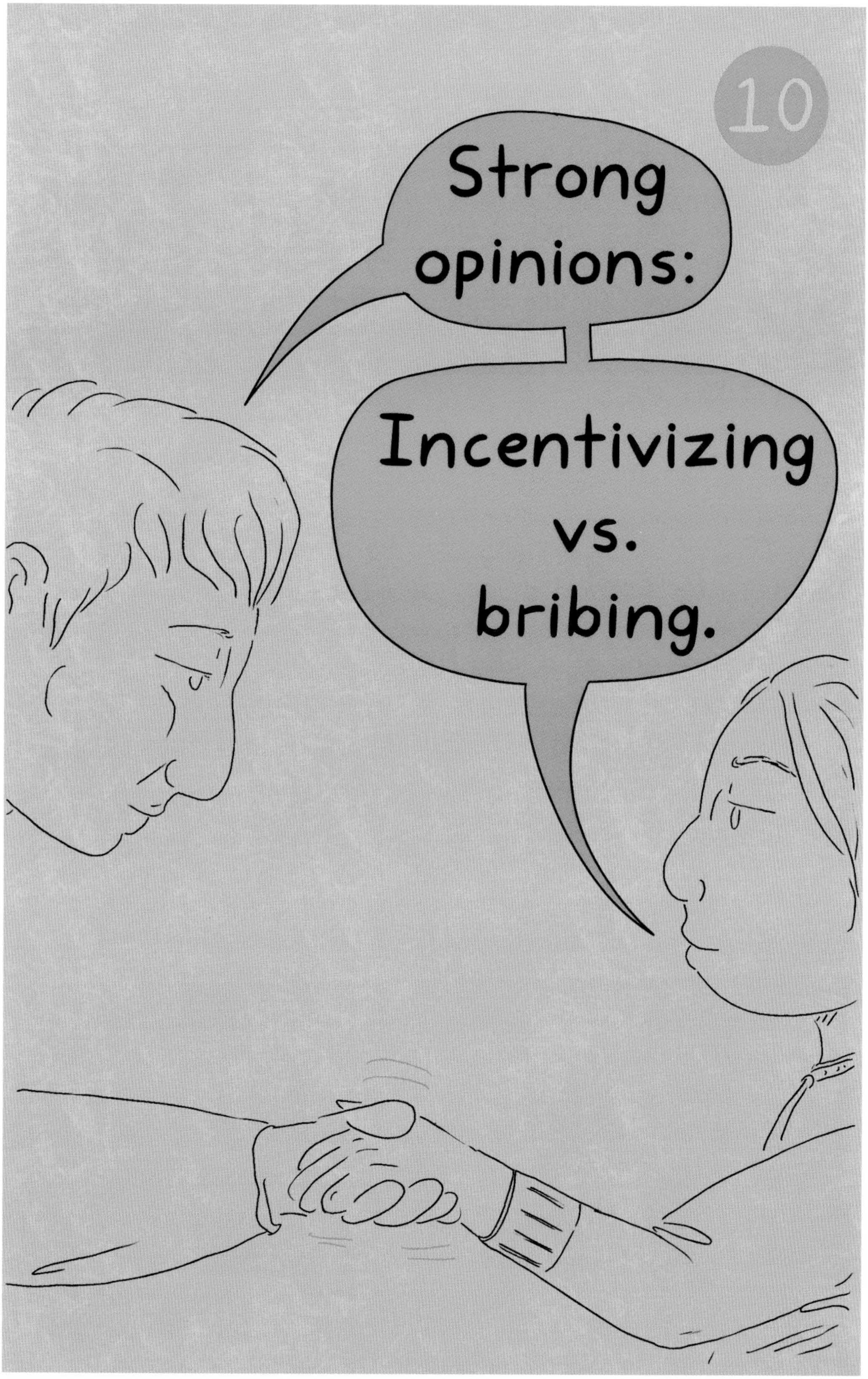
10
Strong opinions:
Incentivizing vs. bribing.

Incentivizing is great, bribing is terrible, and this is the difference:

Incentivizing is a negotiation performed in advance of the situation, in which a parent who has a need and knows they are asking their kids to do something that requires them to stretch their capacity or that there might be some resistance about attempts to sweeten the pot so everyone can feel like they got something they wanted.

If, at the end of a long troop through the butterfly forest, when everyone is sagging a bit, you say,

IF YOU WILL STAND THERE BESIDE THE BUTTERFLY MURAL AND ALLOW ME TO TAKE GRANDPARENT-PLEASING PHOTOS OF YOU WITHOUT MAKING AWFUL FACES OR TRYING TO SABOTAGE ONE ANOTHER, WE CAN GO GET BUBBLE TEA

and they agree to the terms and earn their reward, that is incentivizing.

Child does something parent wants them to do that child finds challenging or is otherwise not into,

and parent provides a minor reward for good performance.

This is useful business, and I recommend it.

Eventually, as they get older, they may try to open negotiations with you in advance of some task or experience they don't love to do, and you can discuss this.

Sometimes the thing has some value to them that they cannot appreciate yet,

and sometimes you will find their request is fair.

I AM NOT LETTING YOU STAY UP AN EXTRA HALF-HOUR IN EXCHANGE FOR YOUR ATTENDANCE AT HEBREW SCHOOL. YOU ARE THERE TO LEARN ABOUT OUR RELIGION AND CULTURE, AND THAT IS ITS OWN REWARD.

YES, IF YOU WATCH YOUR SISTER WHILE I AM PICKING THE CAT UP FROM THE VET, I WILL ALSO PICK UP COOKIES, AND IF EVERYONE IS STILL ALIVE AND NOTHING IS BROKEN WHEN I RETURN, YOU CAN HAVE THEM.

There's also eventually the part where you can say,

YOU'RE RIGHT, I HAVE SOMETIMES OFFERED TO GET YOU A TREAT IF YOU FOCUSED ON BEING PATIENT WHILE WE WAITED IN LINE FOR AN HOUR AT THE AIRPORT. IT WAS RIGHT AT THE EDGE OF YOUR CAPACITY AND I NEEDED TO KEEP YOU ON THE SUNNY SIDE OF THAT. NOW I'M HOPING YOU ARE OLD ENOUGH TO HAVE BUILT THE PATIENCE TO DO IT WITHOUT NEEDING TO SHAKE ME DOWN FOR GUMMY WORMS TO GET THROUGH.

(Although if we are being completely honest, I always have gummy worms at the airport.)

Bribing is what happens when things have <u>already</u> gone south and you're standing next to the huge butterfly sculpture, people are queuing impatiently behind you with their own restless children, and one of your kids is in hiding behind a wing so only their cowlick and one shoe is in the photo, the other one attempting to turn their eyelids inside out, while you ask them repeatedly and with increasing urgency to PLEASE STOP—

and then, in desperation, you say,

PLEASE, IF YOU STAND STILL FOR ONE MINUTE, I WILL TAKE YOU TO GET BUBBLE TEA.

That is bribing, and you don't want to go down that road, because it leads to children who have it reinforced that if they act up, fail to listen, or misbehave, they will eventually get a treat. Which is, I am guessing, and I think my guess is good, not what you want to teach them. Sometimes you will just have to skip the photo

or leave the restaurant

or let them wail on the floor in the customs hall while you speak soothingly and pet their hair and offer distractions.

(Sometimes it may not feel safe to do that. Some of us cannot run the risk of official attention. In which case, you do what you need to do for your own and your child's safety, and don't listen to anyone who tells you otherwise.)

It doesn't feel great, and of course you can try to break the cycle and get them positively engaged by asking them to draw you a picture or stand on one foot.

Promising them a treat if they can do a hard thing well enough is a fine and noble practice, and frankly we do it for ourselves and our friends all the time. Rewarding success, especially success that's hard won, is a great parenting choice.

But offering them a treat to stop doing something they know they shouldn't do, even if they're completely dysregulated and can't help it, isn't doing anyone any favours—though you can and should give them your attention, love, and help in those moments rather than set phasers on ignore.

SPECIAL NOTE:

If they've lost their shit and cannot find it again, you can help them co-regulate with things like

breathing together

or singing a song

or reading a book aloud,

or sometimes you can distract them with silliness like putting nonsense on your head

or producing something absorbing like a little toy they like.

Sometimes it's just too much, and you have to stop everything and get them some food or a nap before you can continue.

You may end up being the one who needs a treat when it's all over, and I would like to say, for the record, that you absolutely fucking deserve it, friend.

When they're small, you can teach them two or three things, and that's it, so choose wisely.

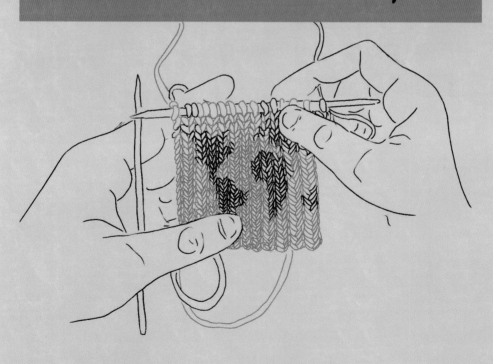

Recently, on a long trip, we went to the Los Angeles County Museum of Art to see an exhibit called Afro-Atlantic Histories.

We all like looking at art, and we spent two hours there. The children peppered my husband and me constantly with questions and prompts about the work—

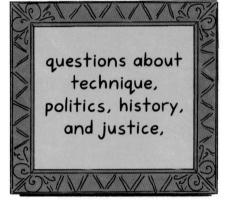

questions about technique, politics, history, and justice,

questions with follow-up questions ranging from the alarmingly specific

WHY IS HE ONLY CRYING ON ONE SIDE?

to the utterly fantastical.

DO YOU THINK IF I STOOD STILL LONG ENOUGH SOMEONE MIGHT THINK I WAS A SCULPTURE?

It was lovely, and truly everything we hoped for when we got into this parenting business, but by the end, my husband and I were exhausted from two hours of explain-o-matic.

But when we got in the car to leave (to go get lilikoi slushes and play on the playground for a while), we caught each other's eye and smiled, and he said,

Their curiosity about absolutely everything is sometimes overwhelming, but it is also one of our core values.

I find that this is a good way to think about what qualities you really, dearly want to cultivate in your children—and it cannot be more than two or three, because these are the ones you never, ever, ever let slide.

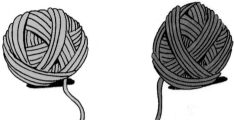

That you remind and correct and discuss every time, without fail. The ones that underpin the person you most hope they are in the world. These are the qualities you model as often as possible, that you narrate the values behind as you make your choices, so that they become inextricably entwined with the way your children understand you and see the world.

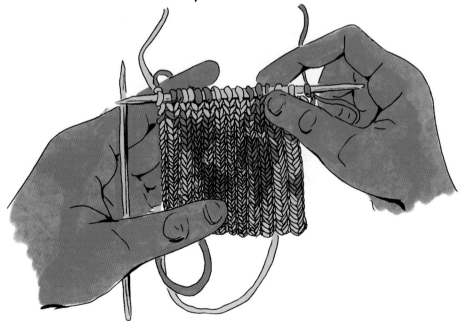

I did not understand this before we had children, but we fumbled forward anyhow and managed to raise these children who are, first, last, and always,

KIND AND — CURIOUS AND — COMMITTED TO JUSTICE.

The satisfaction of this carries me through the fact that they're

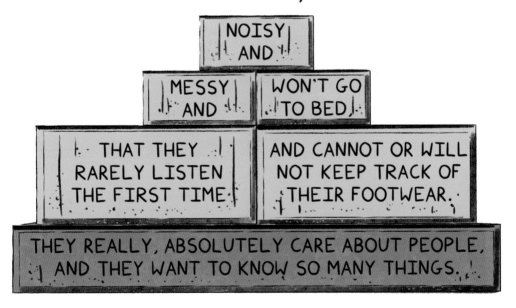

NOISY AND

MESSY AND — WON'T GO TO BED,

THAT THEY RARELY LISTEN THE FIRST TIME — AND CANNOT OR WILL NOT KEEP TRACK OF THEIR FOOTWEAR.

THEY REALLY, ABSOLUTELY CARE ABOUT PEOPLE, AND THEY WANT TO KNOW SO MANY THINGS.

They want to know more things than I know, that's for sure, and that's speaking as a person who once subjected his children and their random friend to a ten-minute impromptu lecture on the etymology of the word "city" on the way home from the trampoline park.

...AND SO "CIVIS" REFERRED TO PEOPLE, RATHER THAN PLACE...

They also will not stand for even a second of someone else's bigotry, even when it would be safer to let it slide. (Ask me sometime about the day I got a call from a parent to inform me that my child had picked up

an entire bench

to defend their child from some gender-inflected violence and to thank them for it, a situation that my child had not bothered to even mention.)

So perhaps this is a good time (no matter how old your kiddos are) for all relevant adults to think forward into the future of this person and imagine what qualities matter more to you than any others, enough that you will never ever "just let it go,"

enough that these qualities will give you something to hang on to during the times you discover that the laundry you carefully folded has been dumped on the floor in a heap and the dog has lain upon it;

or the times you watch, horrified, as they walk in their wet, muddy boots across the floor;

or the times they scream and run from you as though you are trying to remove their eyeballs with a grapefruit spoon, to the point that multiple strangers look over with concern, when in fact you are trying to put a hat on them, you absolute monster.

Think forward into the future of them.
Think of them at ten, at twenty, at forty,

and try to imagine the person you hope to have raised—

how they respond to adversity, to change, to opportunity, to whatever circumstances that amount of time will bring.

Imagine how you would most want them to behave if they made a major mistake,

if someone was in trouble,

if they hurt someone's feelings or someone hurt theirs.

Do you want them to be great
negotiators or problem solvers or planners or fixers?

Consider how you hope they will deal with

disappointment,   obstruction,   grief,

joy,   pleasure,   success.

When you think about work, do you want them to be

wealthy   or   or   or to feel like
     accomplished   happy   they're making
                                   a difference

(rarely all possible at once)?

Start there, consider which two or three of your values will help them to get there, and then model them and talk about them and discuss them and bring them into absolutely everything. And then, you hope for the best.

When I originally wrote the above paragraph,
I included the line

SQUINT AND IGNORE THE REALITIES OF CLIMATE CHANGE FOR THIS PURPOSE, PLEASE.

And then my husband reminded me that as more things go to shit, we are going to need more thoughtful, engaged people to manage in their absence. That

KIND AND CURIOUS HUMANS WILL BE BETTER ABLE TO CARE FOR EACH OTHER THROUGH ADVERSE WEATHER EVENTS AND CLIMATE CRISES THAN MEAN, GREEDY DULLARDS.

(Did I mention he is very smart?)

Note: I think it's easy to imagine the things children might like (the same things you like!) or what they might wear (the same things you wear! Or wish you could have worn, perhaps)

or what they might enjoy in terms of activities or future work.

I want to encourage you in the strongest possible terms not to do that. You don't know what they will like or wear or be good at or find affirming, or what gender identity or sexual orientation or relationship orientation they may live into. By the time they're grown, the possibilities will probably have expanded anyway.

Imagining them loved and peaceful doesn't require you to fantasize about their heterosexual marriage;

imagining them in work that's fulfilling and with interests that bring them joy doesn't require you to picture them as a surgeon or spending their weekends on the ski slopes.

In fact, the more flexibility you can leave in those future imaginings, the more likely you are to enjoy them when they get there, Gd willing.

In this way you leave the necessary room for your child to be a co-creator of their future, for you to be surprised by them in ways that will delight you both.

You may be a go-go sports family with a kid who loves opera,

or a bunch of economists and political scientists who raise a plumber

(and Gd knows the world needs plumbers).

They may live in a queer polyamorous tangle

or be heterosexual and monogamous,

they may divorce and remarry, they may have children or not. They may work at something non-demanding that pays the bills and save their passion for their hobbies or activism.

The key point here is that all of those choices can be part of a beautiful and fulfilling life, even if they are not what you would have chosen for yourself. That's okay. That may be, in fact, the sign that you are doing a good job. To quote Kahlil Gibran in his work "On Children,"

You may give them your love but not your thoughts,
For they have their own thoughts.
You may house their bodies but not their souls,
For their souls dwell in the house of tomorrow,
    which you cannot visit, not even in your dreams.
You may strive to be like them, but seek not to make
    them like you.
For life goes not backward nor tarries with
    yesterday.
You are the bows from which your children as living
    arrows are sent forth.
The archer sees the mark upon the path of the
    infinite, and He bends you with His might that His
    arrows may go swift and far.

As parents, we all think we're the archer. We're doing so many things; surely we are in control of the flight. But really, we're the bow. We have a chance to influence the fletching on our little arrows, to steer and guide them as best we can, but they're the ones who have to fly.

They're the ones who are already flying as soon as they arrive to the outside world.

Be ready to smooth their feathers into the best patterns you know for growth and wellness and joy,

be ready to admire and encourage them,

be ready to help them mend or leave behind any damage that is done to them,

be ready at the beginning to clear the way for them—and then?

Let them fly.

VACATION RULES

A collaborative project by j. wallace skelton, S. Bear Bergman, Shir Bergman, and Solomon Bergman. So far, these rules have held up on many, many kinds of trips, and we offer them in the hope that you might also find them useful.

1. Stay together.

2. Don't fall in a hole.

3. Don't lick anything.

4. Check in before leaving the room.

5. Regular dessert rules do not apply.

6. Regular kicking rules do.

7. Ask after coffee.

12

How we talk about
diversity and difference
at my house.

175

Let me be clear: there are experts in this, and I am not one of them. I have learned from many friends, from many books and other media, and from a lot of trial and error (so much).

In this chapter, I am distilling the work and advice of many beloved people and many good books into the things that have been most helpful in talking to our children about diversity and difference and what we do in our house.

If you're looking for a path to follow, here's one.

① We started immediately.

About half of children's core attitudes about diversity and difference are formed by the time they're three years old, which seems wild on one hand (they just learned what a spoon was!)

but also makes perfect sense; they learn all the words they know and how to operate or understand a shocking number of things from observing and listening. To us.

In this stage, kids are making the building blocks they use to construct an entire world view.

They don't just understand that a handle with a bowl on the end is called "spoon,"

they learn what a spoon is for and where it's used and where it isn't:

Cereal?   Digging in the spider plant?

YES!   NOOOO!

and that it gets washed between uses

and that everyone gets their own

and that they come in different sizes and materials, but all of them operate the same way, and that a spoon isn't recycling when used at home,

even though some other metal or plastic things are recycling

and even though it sometimes is recycling or even trash when eating elsewhere.

They even develop feelings about which spoons they prefer.

Sometimes I too am shocked at how many rules and how much context surrounds even the simplest objects.

Adults forget this because we have known it for so long, which is why we think we can't talk to children about complex things. We forget that their understanding is additive and that every interaction with an object or idea adds layers to their understanding of the thing.

So of course they don't understand ableism after one interaction about it; it takes hundreds— but also it takes hundreds for "spoon."

AND WHEN THEY'VE MASTERED BOTH, THEY'RE READY FOR CHRISTINE MISERANDINO'S SPOON THEORY. I'LL SEE MYSELF OUT.

So of course they're also learning how to think and talk about other people, which is something you can model. Read a book, watch a show, go out in the world and talk to them about how you feel about what you're seeing.

HMM, THERE'S A KID IN THIS BOOK WHO USES WHEELS TO GET AROUND, BUT WE NEVER KNOW HIS NAME, AND HE NEVER SAYS ANYTHING.

I LIKE THIS STORY, BUT I DON'T LIKE THAT CHOICE, BECAUSE I WANT TO KNOW WHAT HE'S DOING AND THINKING TOO.

I LIKE WATCHING A SHOW THAT SHOWS A BLACK GIRL WITH A BLACK MOTHER WHO'S A DOCTOR, BECAUSE WOMEN ONLY GOT TO GO TO MEDICAL SCHOOL ABOUT A HUNDRED YEARS AGO,

AND A LOT OF THOSE SCHOOLS STILL DIDN'T LET BLACK STUDENTS STUDY UNTIL ABOUT SIXTY YEARS AGO, SO THERE AREN'T MANY BLACK WOMEN DOCTORS YET. I THINK IT WILL HELP MORE BLACK GIRLS DECIDE TO BE DOCTORS.

I LOVE THIS POWWOW BECAUSE IT'S RUN BY A TWO-SPIRIT INDIGENOUS GROUP, SO I KNOW WE'LL SEE LOTS OF OTHER PEOPLE WITH OTHER GENDERS DANCING AND PERFORMING.

② We're specific.

There's an idea among parents, I think, that

children aren't born racist or homophobic or ableist or sexist or whatever

(which is true!), but the corollary idea—that

if you don't introduce those ideas, children won't learn them

—is provably false.

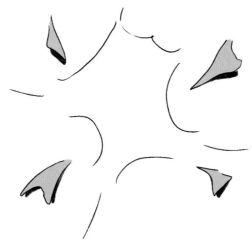

I was on a panel some years ago with Dr. Rebecca Bigler from the University of Texas at Austin, where we discussed how language impacts gender.

Her talk was so smart that I wanted to learn more about her work, and it turned out she was also involved in a number of studies about how white parents of white children talk to their children about race.

and that basically nothing else—

—actually works, because the first five or six years of kid-brain are consumed with categorization and what is like and unlike, and children do naturally express a strong preference for what is visually "like" starting at three months old, unless someone is specific and consistent about disrupting that preference.

So in addition to a lot of media commentary and conversations about things we see in the world, we also talk very specifically about how to interpret what they see.

THERE ARE SOME THINGS YOU CAN'T TELL BY THE COLOUR OF SOMEONE'S SKIN, LIKE IF THEY ARE CLEVER OR FOOLISH, KIND OR THOUGHTLESS, WHAT THEIR INTERESTS MIGHT BE, OR WHAT THEY DO FOR WORK.

BUT YOU CAN TELL GENERALLY WHERE THEIR ANCESTORS ARE FROM AND WHAT EXPERIENCES THEY MIGHT HAVE WITH PEOPLE WHO JUDGE THEM BY THEIR SKIN COLOUR.

SOMEONE WEARING A KIPPAH IS JEWISH,

AND SOMEONE WEARING A HIJAB OR A KUFI IS MUSLIM,

AND SOMEONE WEARING A DASTAAR IS SIKH,

AND THEY WEAR THOSE THINGS TO SHOW THEIR RELIGION. BUT EVEN IF YOU DON'T SEE THOSE THINGS, IT DOESN'T MEAN THAT PERSON IS DEFINITELY NOT JEWISH OR MUSLIM OR SIKH, JUST THAT THEY DON'T CHOOSE TO WEAR RELIGIOUS HEADGEAR.

PEOPLE OF ANY GENDER CAN WEAR THEIR HAIR ANY LENGTH, LIKE YOUR FRIEND KEEWATIN IS A BOY WHO HAS LONG HAIR, AND YOUR FRIEND MARISOL IS A GIRL WHO HAS SHORT HAIR, AND YOU HAVE NON-BINARY FRIENDS AS WELL WITH ALL KINDS OF HAIRSTYLES.

HAIR DOESN'T TELL YOU ABOUT GENDER, IT JUST TELLS YOU WHAT HAIRSTYLE MAKES THAT PERSON FEEL MOST CUTE.

BODIES COME IN ALL SHAPES AND SIZES, AND EVERY BODY IS A GOOD BODY BECAUSE IT GIVES THAT PERSON'S THOUGHTS AND FEELINGS AND IDEAS A PLACE TO RIDE AROUND IN.

SOME PEOPLE MIGHT SAY ONLY THIN BODIES OR STRONG BODIES OR WALKING BODIES ARE GOOD BODIES, BUT ALL BODIES ARE COMPLICATED AND AMAZING AND A LITTLE WEIRD.

Let me acknowledge that this can feel awkward, excessive, or even like massive overkill when talking to a literal baby or toddler.

People may look at you funny or question you for engaging in topics they think are too advanced for so small a person or even scold you for "teaching them to see difference."

But the provable, research-backed fact is that children are literal difference-seeing machines.

It's how they learn to understand the world. What you're doing is giving them context to understand the differences they already see or perceive, instead of letting them draw their own conclusions in a vacuum.

3. We don't talk about, speculate about, or judge other people's bodies or appearances, even if we think they can't hear us.

I continue to be surprised at the number of parents who see nothing wrong with whispering together about someone they think is too fat, or speculating about why someone might be using a mobility device, or carrying on little gestural arguments about a stranger's gender,

and then are shocked when their little Braxton loudly says,

THAT MAN IS SO FAT!

or when EmmaLeigh in Grade 7 takes a photo of someone neurodivergent and shares it on their social media with a mean comment.

They learned it by watching their parents.
They also learn to negatively opine on someone's clothes or hair and conjecture about someone's race or country of origin from their parents, so if you do this?

CUT IT OUT IMMEDIATELY

It sets a terrible example for your children, and also I can guarantee that you are not as slick as you think you are. The person you're making your little guesses or comments about almost certainly knows you're talking about them.

Also: it's impossible to teach a child that they deserve respect and autonomy about their bodies while judging the bodies of other people, so don't do that, please.

4. Pride isn't necessarily the opposite of prejudice, but it can help.

Telling the stories of your own people is especially important when they're erased from (or maligned in) popular media or textbook history, and that's a concept I feel like I instinctively understood.

I also understood that seeking out media that represents my children's experiences was going to be important and that social and cultural contexts in which they could feel part of a majority rather than a minority, as usual, had value

(which is why Jewish summer camps are so popular).

That made sense to me.

What I didn't quite understand because it didn't really apply to us is that family cultural history is valuable for everyone. To be clear: I absolutely do not mean this in a "white pride" way (or "straight pride" or whatever). But if you're Italian or Icelandic or Slovakian or Scottish, and you tell your children stories and the history of your culture and observe cultural practices, it does two things.

One, it disrupts the idea that some people are

and others are

Everyone has an ethnicity, and when kids know that, it gives them both a sense of their own history and culture and a way to understand that everyone has a history and culture worth celebrating.

It also gives you opportunities for cultural exchange and appreciation: invite friends over for Kwanzaa and attend your friends' Feast of Seven Fishes.

You get to enjoy new foods and the opportunity to learn new things together as families, as well as reinforcing the value that it's an honour and a privilege to be invited to share someone's cultural observance.

Two, if you have the benefit of being in a majority group in certain ways (many of us are), you can attend

 or  or

or other performances, events, and celebrations and talk with your children about why they're important.

You can discuss how much of our systems, institutions, legal structures, media, and textbooks reflect your family's majority experience,

protecting you from the extra work of existing in that minority group, and how pleasing it must be for those in the minority to have a day when everything around them reflects their experience.

(Please don't just watch the parade or eat the snacks and call it a happy day, believing that seeing the celebration without having conversation accomplishes something; see #1.)

You can take opportunities in public to address the big and obvious ways marginalization occurs

and note ways that can feel quite subtle if you're not being impacted by them,

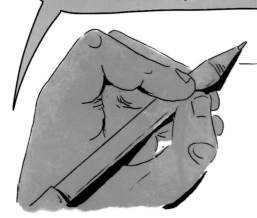

MOTHER'S MAIDEN NAME

as well as noting resonances and similarities.

Cultural celebrations are incredibly fertile places to talk about diversity and difference in positive and accessible ways, while also providing superlative opportunities for snacks and fancy outfits, two things many children love.

Oh Gd, okay. Why is, for example, Queer Pride okay but "Straight Pride" not? Well, here's the thing: all pride movements have developed in opposition to systemic shaming and disempowerment.

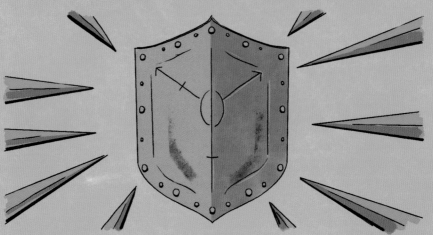

To celebrate your identity is a radical act in a context where the most powerful forces in government, law, education, health care, etc. are busy trying to pretend you don't exist, making your life more difficult, or glossing over whatever genocides they perpetrated or are currently spearheading against your people— and it's a radical act made much easier when people gather in numbers to see and admire but also protect one another.

I understand that certain straight people (and white people, and Christian people) currently feel like they're under attack, but what those people are actually experiencing, while indeed a loss, isn't shaming, erasure, or disempowerment—it's just having to share for the first time. For example,

when 93 percent of all new children's books used to feature a straight white family,

and now it's only 78 percent,

it's true, there is a loss of representation for straight white families. Many straight white people welcome this "loss" because it begins to make room for equity, but some are foolish and therefore mad about it and want things to go back to being 98 percent about them all the time, when they could feel comfortable in their belief that their experience was the only important one and everyone else's were beneath notice. I would like to cordially invite these people, in the vernacular of _my_ people, to go suck the dung out of a dead goat.

The work and words of a number of smart
and thoughtful people contributed to this chapter.
The good ideas all came about from them, or with them.
The not-yet-good ideas are my own.

Mikki Kendall,
author of
Hood Feminism

Dr. Rudine Sims Bishop,
who first articulated
the concept of children's
books as mirrors, windows,
or sliding glass doors

Dr. Ruth Green, MSW,
professor at
York University

Leah Lakshmi
Piepzna-Samarasinha,
author of Care Work and
The Future Is Disabled

Dr. Ibram X. Kendi,
author of How To
Raise an Antiracist

Eli Clare,
author of Exile and Pride
and Brilliant Imperfection

Portia Burch,
on TikTok
as @Portia.Noir

Dr. Abigail Salole,
Director of the EDI
Knowledge Mobilization and
Dissemination Centre at
Sheridan College

Dr. Imani Perry,
author of Breathe:
A Letter to My Sons

Dr. Eve Tuck,
professor at University
of Toronto and Canada
Research Chair of Indigenous
Methodologies with Youth
and Communities

And Angel Adeyoha, Koja Adeyoha,
Candice Fletcher-Pacheco, and Jenn Heiser, whom I am
grateful beyond measure to have learned from in person.

RECIPE FOR JOY:

- One teen
- One car ride at night
- Several hundred thousand pounds of not chastising them for a thoughtfully made choice or attempt that went badly

Add very slowly.

Yield: one shared confidence.

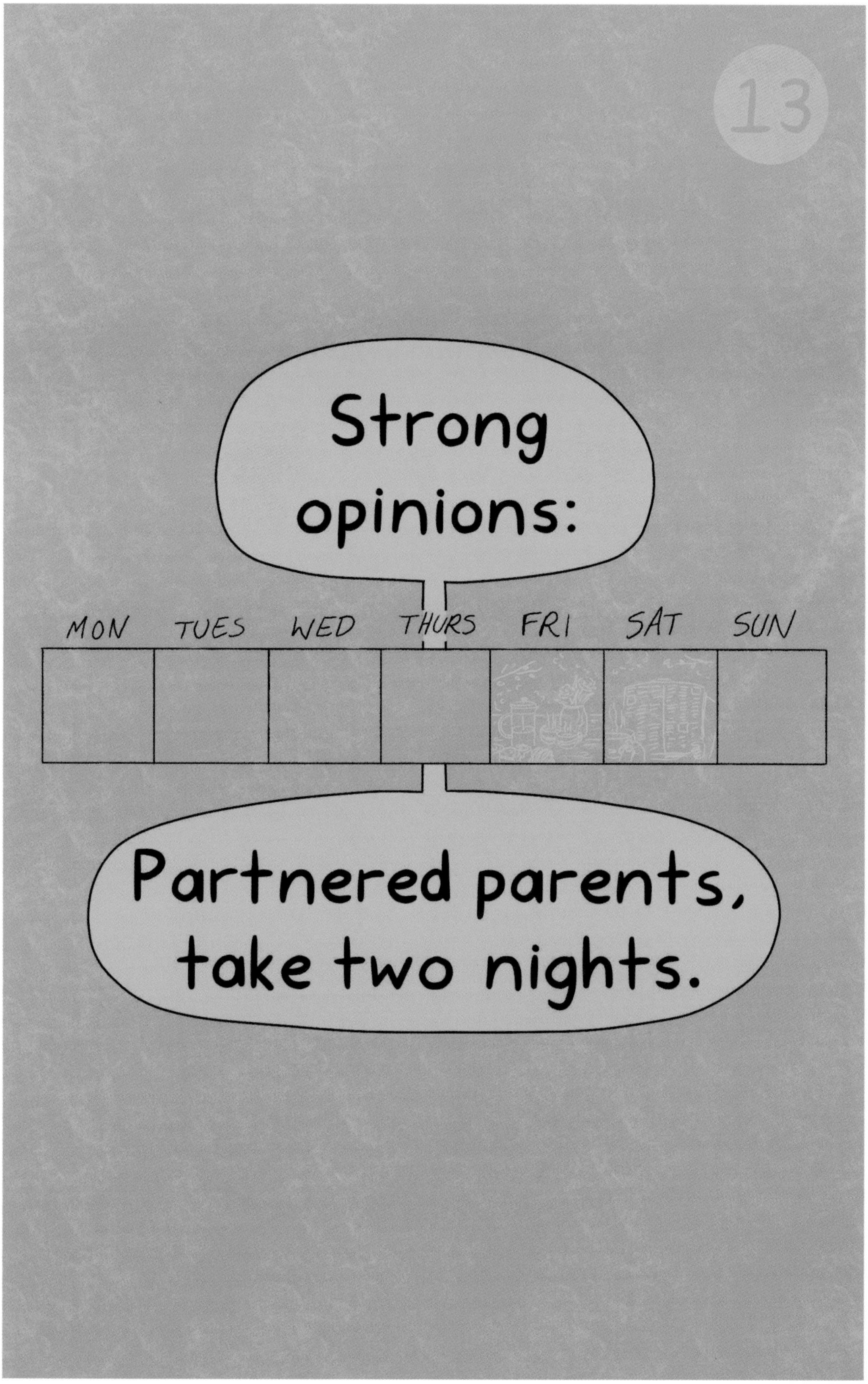
13
Strong opinions:
MON
TUES
WED
THURS
FRI
SAT
SUN
Partnered parents, take two nights.

I remember how excited we were to have an overnight without children the first time, when my in-laws took the kindergartener and the baby, and we just stayed home.

I had plans, friends.

Admittedly they might have been a little ambitious, but they definitely involved

SCHEDULE

☐ Romance

☐ Sex
  ☐ Leisurely sex, not to mention
  ☐ Noisy sex — the kind that's tough to get away with while your children are asleep in the next room

☐ Brunch

Instead, we had a giant fight,

eventually came to an uneasy peace,

slept eleven hours,

and woke up just in time to ransom the children back from my husband's parents, who looked distinctly tired.

I felt disappointed and aggravated with myself
and aggravated with my husband, and then it was
time to resume the million-task schedule that
defines parenting small children.

I told myself we would do it again and
that next time it would be different.

It was not different
the next time.

Or the next,

or the next,

and then something happened: for reasons of traffic and
circumstance, we ended up with a schedule of kid drop-off
on Friday evening to kid collection on Sunday midmorning.

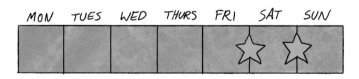

Two nights of child care.

It's not an overstatement to say it was transformative.

We still had a fight the first night, though shorter and less adversarial,

and we still slept like we were an hour from death,

but then we woke up the next morning and did things that were illegal in twenty-three states when I first came out in the early '90s.

Then we had brunch.

Then we sat around and read the paper and sipped our second coffees,

and we still did not accomplish any of the chores that we'd imagined we might.

The second night, we indulged ourselves in various ways,

TAKEOUT!

EDIBLES!

REALITY TELEVISION!

then went to bed early and lay together,

talking and making each other laugh

and being close and sweet on each other.

We woke up feeling great.

So here's my recommendation: if you can trade sleepovers or send the kids to someone's relatives or whatever child-care arrangement feels within your budget, you may be better off doing it less often but taking two nights.

Know going in that the first one is probably just for finishing every fight that got interrupted by child needs before you could reach resolution and repair and getting a big sleep, and then when you wake up,

there are hours and hours for talking without being interrupted,

for finding your way back to each other as sweethearts and partners,

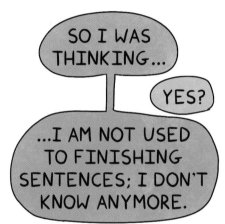

SO I WAS THINKING...

YES?

...I AM NOT USED TO FINISHING SENTENCES; I DON'T KNOW ANYMORE.

for all the good stuff outside of parenting so you can return with renewed energy to the pleasures of your children.

Also, friends, do not allow anyone to make you feel guilty about this! If they even begin to try, remind them that happy and connected sweethearts make happy and connected parents. And then stop listening.

14

Swears vs. slurs,
and other notes
on language:
a letter.

Dear Brave Correspondent,

> We live in a world where there are so much more vile and ugly things than profanity.
>
> —David Draiman, lead singer of Disturbed

In our house, we don't talk about "bad words." We divide them into two distinct categories: swears and slurs.

Swears are all the words George Carlin warned us about, and I think probably we are a little flexible on this category because it isn't a huge issue in our house. Neither of the adults is particularly inclined toward swear words in our regular speech, nor are any of the adults with whom the kids spend significant time. Swears, in our family, fall into a category that we have defined as "things you can begin to experiment with after you turn thirteen." For reference, other items in this category include beer, coffee, and having your own phone.

YOU MUST BE THIS TALL

I'm not under the impression that my children never swear when they are away from us, but they have the good sense and common courtesy not to swear in front of their parents or any adults that their parents know, and frankly, that is enough for me. I don't have a lot of strong feelings in any direction about swearing, except that sometimes it's necessary, and the Scottish are exceptionally good at it.

INCOMPREHENSIBLE JIZZTRUMPET!

Slurs are a different story. We define a slur as "any word whose purpose is to demean or degrade a group of people." We do not say them, ever, unless we are using them to describe ourselves in a reclaiming way, a right that other people hold to their own locations of identity.

Then we do the work about equity and justice to back it up; we are not saying a more acceptable word with unpleasantness behind it and calling it good. This isn't a lesson in manners but a question of making sure children know what these words mean and what ugliness underlies them, so when they encounter them in the world, they know right away what they're dealing with and what to do about it—say

(or sexist, antisemitic, fatphobic, etc.)—because we are also not raising them to stand idly by while someone else perpetuates ugliness.

Start as soon as your child encounters swears in the wild and appears to take notice that something interesting has happened. For a while they won't, because they're still figuring out how language works, but eventually you'll see on their faces when they look over at you that they know someone has said something that is somehow incorrect.

(Unless you are all a notably sweary bunch and your kid has no sense of which words might be the "bad words," in which case just start at three or so with the slurs part. People sometimes have extremely dire predictions about these children being unable to manage adult life without dropping f-bombs every five seconds, but it mostly seems to work out fine.)

Also, while we're here, your children will model their own language (and therefore, to some degree, their view of the world) on yours.

Do you say, "illegal alien" or ("undocumented immigrant")?

Do you describe someone's face as "deformed" or ("unusual")?

Do you say, "pro-life" or ("anti-choice")?

"prostitute" or ("sex worker")?

You get the point, I'm sure—your children will describe people the way you describe them, so upgrade your vocabulary to match your values, if you haven't already. (To start you off, in case you're uncertain, the latter item in each of the above pairs is the language we use in our house.)

This might also be a time to think a little more critically about descriptive words. Oppressive language may have crept into your vernacular without you noticing. Perhaps, if you ever say these things, it's time to let go of "gypped," which is a slur against Roma people; or "wheelchair-bound," which is the literal opposite of the experience of most people who use wheels, as their wheelchair is a primary location of their freedom to move around in the world; or "Indian summer," which references the idea that Indigenous people, historically, would offer the loan of something, misinterpreted by colonizers as it being given, and then expect it to be returned when or if it wasn't needed anymore, giving rise to the term "Indian giver." You can teach yourself not to describe things you find boring or unpleasant as "lame" or experiences that are wild, intense, or upsetting as "crazy."

And don't get me started on the number of things that are mistakenly described as Chinese, including "Chinese jump rope," "Chinese checkers," "Chinese handcuffs," and so on (known in our house as a circular jump rope, star checkers—the game is actually a simplified version of a German game called Star Halma—and finger cuffs), all of which were brought to the American market during a period of Orientalist interest in things considered "exotic."

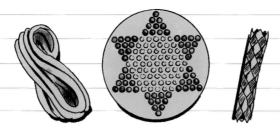

You don't have to turn yourself into the Language Police if that's not your bent, but the more you refrain from using terms that reference actual people and groups unkindly—even if those words are common in your circles—the easier it becomes to make a habit of speaking positively (or negatively!) about people based on the qualities they've cultivated or the actions they've taken rather than something about their body or identity.

love and courage,
Bear

15

Talk to them all the time, about everything.

Our youngest was seven when someone asked him,

DO YOU KNOW WHAT DRUGS ARE?

YES,

he replied promptly, while eating a freezie.

METH IS THE SCARIEST DRUG.

SOME DRUGS YOUR DOCTOR GIVES YOU, BUT SOME YOU BUY FOR YOURSELF.

AND YOU SHOULD ONLY TRY NEW DRUGS WITH OLD FRIENDS.

AND SOME PEOPLE WHO HAVE TO LIVE OUTSIDE BECAUSE THEY DON'T HAVE MONEY FOR A HOUSE NEED THEM BECAUSE IT'S REALLY HARD TO LIVE OUTSIDE.

I'll be honest: I found his answer pleasing. Slightly jumbled up in the way of a seven-year-old and certainly lacking some complexity, but he hit several critical highlights.

The person who'd asked the question looked shocked. She later related that she (an elementary educator herself) wasn't upset by the content but was startled by the level of nuance. She'd expected D.A.R.E-style

"DRUGS KILL. SAY NO TO DRUGS"

messaging, and so she asked us how we had gotten a child who is completely lovely but frankly not the most practical to retain several key harm reduction messages about drug use.

It took some reverse engineering to understand it, but the method here stems from the idea that you never want to have just one Big Talk with a kid about anything important.

HARM REDUCTION

You want to discuss it a zillion times, directly and obliquely, starting very early.

My experience is that we feel fine about that with some things, but with topics that seem overwhelming

we prefer to wait because it seems like a lot.
The problem is, that doesn't really work.

Kids internalize values through repetition. That's why people attend school daily, religious services weekly, sports practices three times a week.

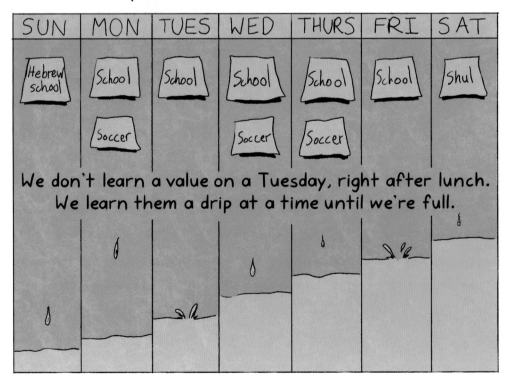

SUN	MON	TUES	WED	THURS	FRI	SAT
Hebrew school	School	School	School	School	School	Shul
	Soccer		Soccer	Soccer		

We don't learn a value on a Tuesday, right after lunch.
We learn them a drip at a time until we're full.

So talking to kids a lot about values makes it much more likely that they'll share yours. But, uh, how do we do that? If your kids go to religious school, they probably get an hour or two a week of values education, but even that isn't very much. It's hard to sit a three-year-old down for a good old-fashioned values talk.

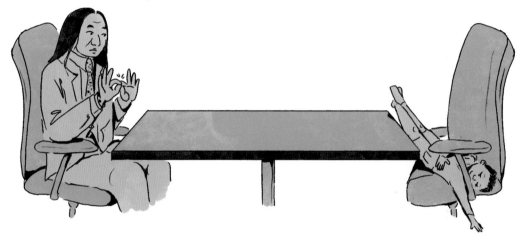

But the values we teach our children are the lenses through which they will understand every new person, question, and idea they encounter, and they are aware of both encounters and newness starting before they're three months old.

So how are these many useful conversations supposed to happen? Are we meant to just invent them out of thin air?

I figured out what we did by sort of piecing it together in retrospect:

This is one way. There are surely other ways, but we have found this one easy to integrate without adding steps, and that, I think, is the kind of intervention parents deeply need.

Step 0: Start way sooner than you think you need to.

Birth is fine, actually.

HI.

They're not going to be replying to you for a while, but they are listening, so talk to them.

OH? WHAT DO YOU THINK?

Talk for the value of their hearing language, for the soothing quality of their parent's voice, and also to get them accustomed to it as a ritual.

Step 1: Let go of your concern that any topic might be too complex for a child to know about. Also let go of the idea that you need to explain everything perfectly. Just set those concerns down gently and drive off, like you're releasing a mouse you've caught into a meadow miles from home—no need for murder, but out you get.

Step 2: Find discussion topics. The most common way in our family is listening to the news together, but what we see while we're out driving or walking, what we're reading, etc., is fair game.

Add movies, television, video games, sports—whatever you watch or listen to.

Step 3 (if you feel familiar with and up-to-date on what's being discussed): Talk to them about what you hear or see.

Don't be afraid to express your frustration with bad political news or your approval of less-bad news and, should you encounter any in the wild, actual good news.

> I AM SO TIRED AND I HATE THIS SO MUCH. I WISH A THOUSAND PLAGUES UPON THE STATE.

> OH, THAT IS LOVELY. PEOPLE WORKED VERY HARD TO MAKE THAT HAPPEN.

Ask if they understand what's happening and why you feel that way about it, and if they don't, explain. They may not have a lot of feelings about the news yet, which is fine. You're sharing your values and helping them develop theirs, plus you're teaching them that discussion is a great way to learn.

Be learners together!

Use the powerful computer most of us now carry in our pockets and figure it out.

Read aloud to them or, when they're old enough, let them read aloud to you while you get the frittata out of the oven or drive the car.

Keep looking stuff up until you feel like you know enough or run out of time.

Do it again the next day, and the next. Sometimes the news will be dull, or you will be, and it will just play in the background and no one will pay it much attention.

That's fine; some days are like that.

Other days you end up late for school because there's a report that pineapples are on backorder in most of North America and you've muttered a little curse, and an alert child pipes in with,

> WHY DO YOU WANT THE DOLE FAMILY TO BE INFESTED WITH THE ITCH OF A THOUSAND FLEAS ON EVERY INCH OF THEIR GENITALS, PAPA?

So now because the pineapple shortage made the news, I'm doing a little impromptu breakfast lecture on the colonization of Hawaii, complete with showing a photo of Sanford Dole so everyone can boo him

and checking what year Queen—

UH, SHE MADE A QUILT IN 'IOLANI PALACE WHERE SHE WAS IMPRISONED, CAN YOU LOOK IT UP? I AM COVERED IN EGGS.

RIGHT, QUEEN LILI'UOKALANI, I'M NOT SURE HOW TO PRONOUNCE IT EITHER, HONEY, LET'S LOOK IT UP.

IN THE MIDDLE THERE? THAT'S THE GLOTTAL STOP. OKAY, WHAT DID YOU FIND FOR PRONUNCIATION? THAT DOESN'T SOUND RIGHT, WHO MADE THIS VIDEO? LET'S FIND A HAWAIIAN SAYING IT.

I KNOW THE APOSTROPHE IN THE MIDDLE IS A GLOTTAL STOP. A GLOTTAL STOP IS WHEN YOUR VOCAL CHORDS ALL COME TOGETHER AND STOP YOUR BREATH FOR A SECOND AND IT MAKES A LITTLE PAUSE IN THE WORD. LIKE WHEN YOU SAY "UH-OH."

OHHHH, OKAY, THAT'S ABOUT THE CELEBRATION OF HER BIRTHDAY. LET'S LISTEN. HANG ON, PAUSE.

DID SHE SAY THAT MAI POINA MEANS "DON'T FORGET"? THE MAI POINA WALKING TOUR TO TEACH PEOPLE ABOUT HAWAIIAN SOVEREIGNTY AND HISTORY? THAT'S THE SAME AS JEWS SAYING "ZACHOR" ABOUT THE HOLOCAUST. IT MEANS "REMEMBER" IN HEBREW, AND...

OH SHIT, IT'S 8:30. FIND YOUR SHOES, WE HAVE TO GO.

Step 5: Don't worry about repeating yourself.

They were only half listening half of the times anyhow,

and the other half, less than that.

Kids rehear you and have different questions at every age and stage,

WHY ISN'T THERE SCHOOL TODAY?

WHAT ARE THE TEACHERS ASKING FOR THAT THE PREMIER DOESN'T WANT TO GIVE?

HOW CAN THE UNION SUPPORT TEACHERS WHEN THEY DON'T ALL WANT THE SAME THING?

and frankly, considering how quickly they can enter and exit a truly consuming phase, you could probably hit all the highlights once a week, if you wanted to.

Step 6: Cheat a little if you need to.

Are you feeling like it's time to revisit consent education? Harm reduction? Empathy and support? Queue up a movie or podcast or book or artwork that gives you the jumping-off point you need to discuss that thing.

But to be honest, I have found that the weekday news on CBC (or whatever the local public radio station is, if we're travelling) provides most of what we need.

Step 7: Don't be afraid to screw it up. If you made a mistake last week? Fix it today.

WHO?

Did you say

GLORIA STEINEM

when you meant to say

GERTRUDE STEIN?

That happens.
Being imperfect but curious gives your kids the latitude to also feel like it's okay to be imperfect but curious, and that, in my opinion, is parenting gold.

RECIPE FOR JOY:

- One child
- One TikTok recipe
- Many repetitions of encouragement
- A hearty pinch of willingness to help with cleanup

Combine gently with offers of assistance.

Yield: one feeling of accomplishment and one meal you didn't have to cook.

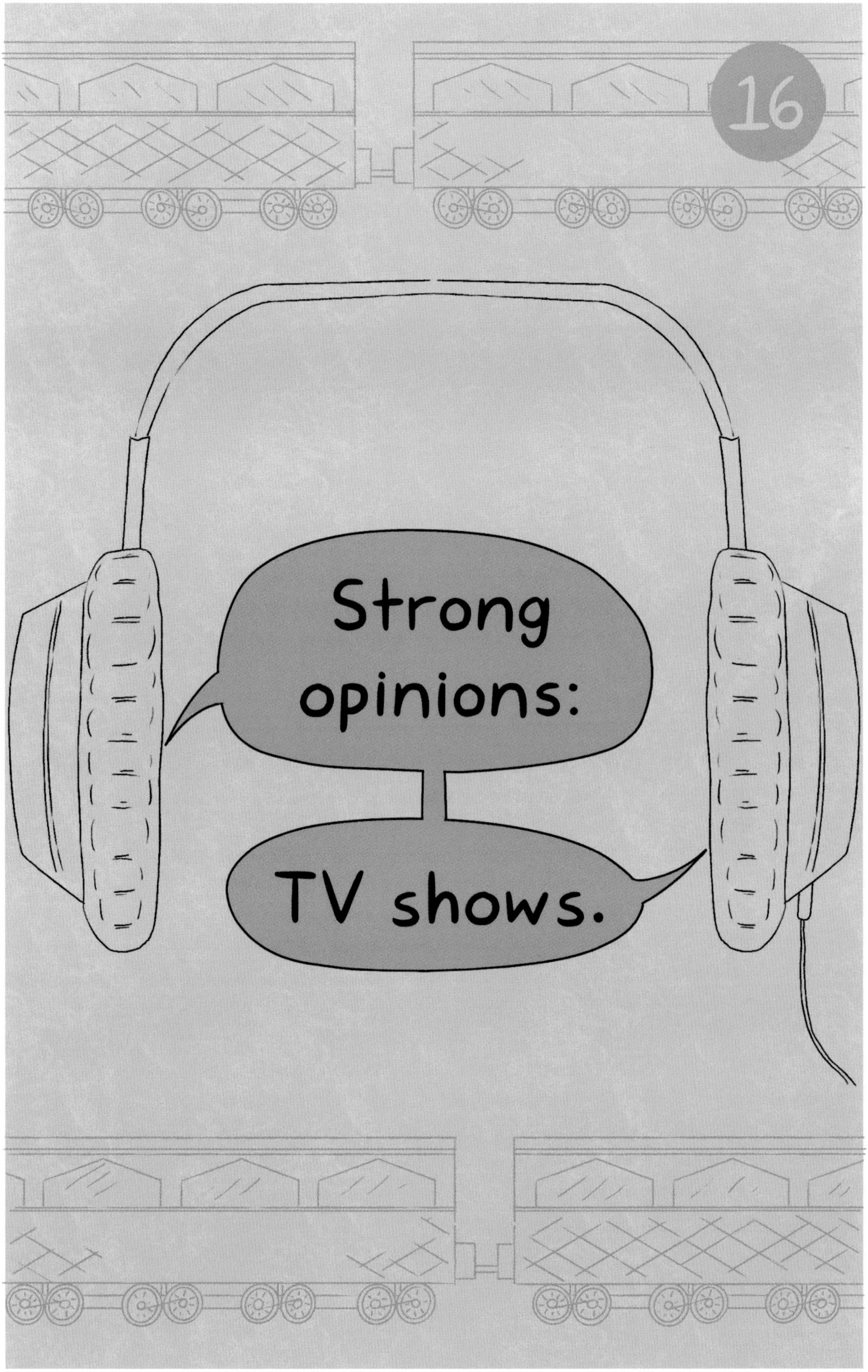
16
Strong opinions:
TV shows.

The Octonauts has the same vibes as PAW Patrol, but Octonauts is so much better; animals solve problems using wild technology in both, but Octonauts has much better science and much less copaganda, as well as girl scientists, plural.

<u>Dinosaur Train</u>, while a little kumbaya on the topic of whether vegetarian dinos and obligate carnivore dinos could get along, does a really great job with two things my household values:

the excitement of going somewhere new,

making friends with the people(saurs) who live there,

 and checking out how they do things (and what they eat);

and the idea that not everything has to be fun in the same way for everyone.

Sometimes the neurodivergent dinosaur who likes tending his collections and who gets nervous when plans are too uncertain simply stays home from an adventure if he's not feeling into it, and no one minds—

sometimes they bring him back cool stuff for his collection.

The Muppet Show has held up remarkably well.

Also, it's a show about making a show, by people who have a lot of enthusiasm but...

...varying amounts of skill, and that's a vibe I will always enjoy.

YEAH, LIKE AN ARMED ROBBERY!

Thomas and Friends is a terrible show in which the plot of every episode is that some train is being an asshole for twenty-and-a-half minutes, and then eventually someone tells that train they're being awful and to stop.

They do stop, and typically they say sorry, but I don't want my children watching terrible behaviour for most of the time.

No <u>Caillou.</u>
Ever.

If you have junior nerd children or hope to make them, consider some podcasts too. There are really good kids' podcasts, some of which are educational (<u>Homeschool History</u>, <u>But Why</u>) and some of which are just wild flights of imagination (<u>The Story Store</u>, <u>Story Pirates</u>).

Look for podcasts from the assorted public radio / public broadcasting projects of various countries, like PBS, NPR, CBC, BBC, and so on for a place to start.

 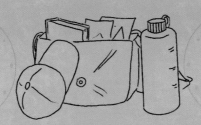 

17

On transitions and how hard they are.

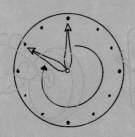 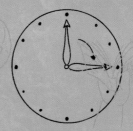

I am aware of how this looks, but I don't mean the transgender kind; I mean the kind where you have to

stop doing what you're doing,

prepare your things and your body to leave,

and actually go.

It's impossible to explain how much time, energy, will, and patience parents spend managing transitions, but it's a lot.

A ridiculous amount, even when kids are transitioning from nothing in particular to something fun. Transitions are very challenging.

This is normal.

What's more, some kids naturally get better at it with some help and scaffolding,

and some just become adults who are constantly late for everything

because they don't fully understand what's required to leave a place and how long each of those things takes, to wit:

Come to a stopping place in what you're doing.

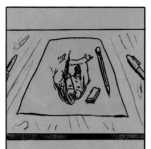

Put it down or away.

Change the position of your body, if relevant.

Assess whether you need to use the washroom.

Find your shoes and any outerwear or gear you may require.

Find your bag, if any.

Consider what you need for the next evolution, if anything.

Put whatever you need for the next evolution into your bag (water bottle, mask, book, keys, wallet, phone, tiny cars, plastic frogs, emergency granola bars, deck of cards, important rocks, tiara, whatever).

Put on your shoes and whatever else you need to leave the house.

Pick up your bag.

Leave the house.

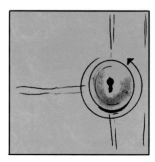

This does not even include

picking an outfit,   doing your hair,   or applying makeup,

to say nothing of knock-on effects like picking a great outfit but then realizing your nail polish clashes and must be changed,

or realizing you need to wear your grandmother's brooch on this occasion for sentimental reasons and therefore ransacking your jewellery box in a panic to look for it before recalling that it's still on your tweed blazer, uh, for example.

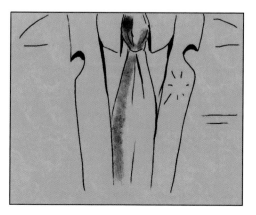 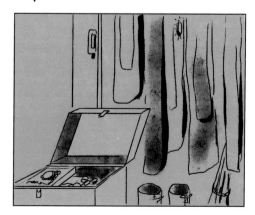

Here are three tips to manage transitions that sometimes make me feel fractionally less stabby:

①. Know your family's Leave-Go Gap.

Every person has their own Leave-Go Gap. It's the amount of time between when someone knows

IT'S TIME TO LEAVE

and when they are actually ready to go, as in to walk out the door.

Some people have a very long Leave-Go Gap,

and some people's are quite short.

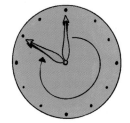

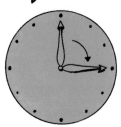

It really depends on how much they're thinking ahead, how easy it is for them to stop working, how many things they typically bring with them on an outing, how likely they are to get distracted in the process of putting their stuff together, and how much external processing they typically require about what's needed next. What you need to understand here is how long it takes between when you say,

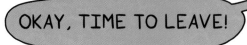

OKAY, TIME TO LEAVE!

and when everyone in your household is ready to go.

Absolutely no femme-shaming is permitted in this process. If you ever like it when someone looks cute, then do not discourage the time cuteness takes.

And if you've ever been rescued with the safety pin or Tide pen or ibuprofen or change or Band-Aid or lube or granola bar someone has produced from their purse, you don't get to huffily act like packing a purse is a frivolity taking up valuable time.

Femme business is sacred, and what we are not going to do is shame our femme loved ones for taking time to do the exact things we value when they're finished, vershteh?

Sometimes there's no way to shorten a particular individual or group's Leave-Go Gap very much; you just have to know what it is so you can start early enough. Sometimes people will try to fight you about this and tell you that if you don't need to be there until one, there's no need to leave at noon. I will confess to you that I have not been above getting out the stopwatch in these situations and showing them exactly how long it takes for everyone to move from "time to leave" to actually going.

❷ Beware of Lestering.

I don't even remember why we call it this, but in my household, "Lestering" is any activity that you might do while you're Ready To Go and waiting for someone else who is still in their Leave-Go Gap.

This is really more of an adult issue, but adults are part of the household transition picture. If not all adults are participating in the leave-taking, it's always more complicated. Recommended: unless it's unavoidable, all grown-ups on hand should help with getting the kids to the Go point. Somehow, if some adults are in view but not working on Project Go, it's harder to manage the transition even if everyone has been advised that that adult is working on their Nobel Prize acceptance speech and cannot be disturbed.

We had to give it a name because it turned out that my husband would see me sitting and typing and would therefore think there was no rush to get his stuff together because I was still working, or sometimes vice versa. Lestering complicates transitions because it's easy for two (or more, see next) people to both think,

IF THEY'RE STILL READING, I HAVE PLENTY OF TIME

and then half an hour has passed. The way around this is to announce,

I'M READY TO GO. I AM JUST LESTERING.

That way, everyone else engaged with the process knows that's what's happening.

KEY POINT:

If you make this announcement,

 you must have all your things in your bag,

 you must already have used the washroom,

 you must already have found
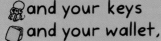your glasses
and your keys
and your wallet,

 and you must be ready to put your feet in your shoes and walk out the door.

Otherwise, you get...

❸ The Law of Exponential Tardiness

Have you ever tried to get a group of people together to go out to dinner? Perhaps you're meeting in the hotel lobby or at a bar from which you will proceed to dinner,

and one person shows up on time,

then another person shows up almost on time,

then you're waiting for person number three, so person number one decides they will

QUICKLY RUN TO THE WASHROOM,

during which time person number three arrives and joins the waiting,

whereupon person number two sees someone across the room they would like to have a quick word with while you wait for person number one,

and I'm sure you see where this is going.

Nowhere, is where it's going.

Especially not to dinner in time for your reservation.

In order to manage this during your parenting transitions, you need to accustom your children as early as possible to the idea that sometimes they will simply need to wait a moment and not be doing anything.

They will just have to stand quietly, or sit quietly, with their bag in their hands and their shoes on, until everyone else is ready to walk out the door. Ideally, without complaint or too much fidgeting, but we will take what we can get. (Often what we get are children who suddenly discover, when they tune in to their bodies for half a second instead of their show or project or book or whatever, that they are HUNGRY or now NEED TO PEE even though they swore they weren't or didn't. Be prepared: this is also part of the Leave-Go Gap, and you will just have to account for it until they're grown enough to account for it themselves.)

They will hate this and generally resist it at all costs.

Children are constitutionally opposed to waiting.
When there is nothing to do, they will naturally try to
wander away and seek entertainment, which often takes
the form of poking whomever is closest.

It's not even that much their fault; it's a very busy and
curious time of life, and waiting without complaint is a
skill that must be cultivated.

It may take many, many reminders that they just need to stand and wait for a moment. I'm sorry to report that this is extremely typical, and though your mileage may vary, it probably will not vary much. If your family finds transitions a particular challenge, allot more time and/or try to reduce the number of them.

Do they really need to come into the house, or can you just meet them off the school bus with a snack and wave them directly into the car?

Are you sure you have to do a few errands on the way home with them in the car, or could they just stay and play on the school playground and be collected an hour later, after you have erranded?

But overall, transitions are rough for a long time, so
1) try to help everyone improve, but
2) also don't let a great trip or outing end in unpleasantness because the transition out of it was hard.

Transitions are hard, regardless. Give them a separate part of your feelings-place and don't let how much they suck ruin the other fun things you got to do, if you can help it. Pro tip: name it out loud, as in,

> WE HAD SO MUCH FUN ON OUR TRIP TO THE STRONG MUSEUM, AND THEN THE TRANSITION FROM THE HOTEL TO THE CAR REALLY MADE ME WANT TO RUN AWAY FROM HOME AND CHANGE MY NAME, BUT THAT'S TRANSITIONS FOR YOU.

They're still awfully challenging, though. Sorry, friend. It's not your fault.

RECIPE FOR JOY:

- One child
- One doughnut
- One family brunch
- Eleven thousand opportunities to model generosity

Stir until fully combined (may take years).

Yield: one child who takes a bite of something wonderful and then says, THIS IS DELICIOUS. TRY SOME!

The absolute least I could stand to write about gender roles, gender expectations, and heteronormativity.

18

Let me be honest:
I was not going to write a chapter about parenting and gender. But everyone with whom I discussed this plan looked at me sideways and said some version of

FRIEND, YOU TEACH PEOPLE ABOUT GENDER FOR A LIVING.

Which is true, but this is the problem: I have too many Strong Opinions about gender. I got completely overwhelmed by the idea of trying to distill them into just a few pages—especially right now, with what feels like the whole world yelling into my inbox about how trans people are making children trans (as if that's the worst thing a child could be, never mind the fact that it's impossible).

So, okay. What are the most important parts?

1. Choices for children are critical, and you will have to guard your children's peace around them for a while.

Toys, clothes, activities, hair, accessories, you name it—someone has a gender feeling about it. People will try to correct you if you buy the "wrong" gender of diapers

(they have cartoon characters— some of the cartoons are cars and some of them are princesses, and this is literally for infants).

So part of the job is giving your kiddo a ton of choices in what they want to wear and play with, and another part is pushing back against people who would like to share their unsolicited opinions about that with you.

This means a lot of "yes, and":
dolls and trains and tools and handcrafts and kitchen sets
and superheroes and floofy skirts and knight's helmets,

sports and music and art and dance.

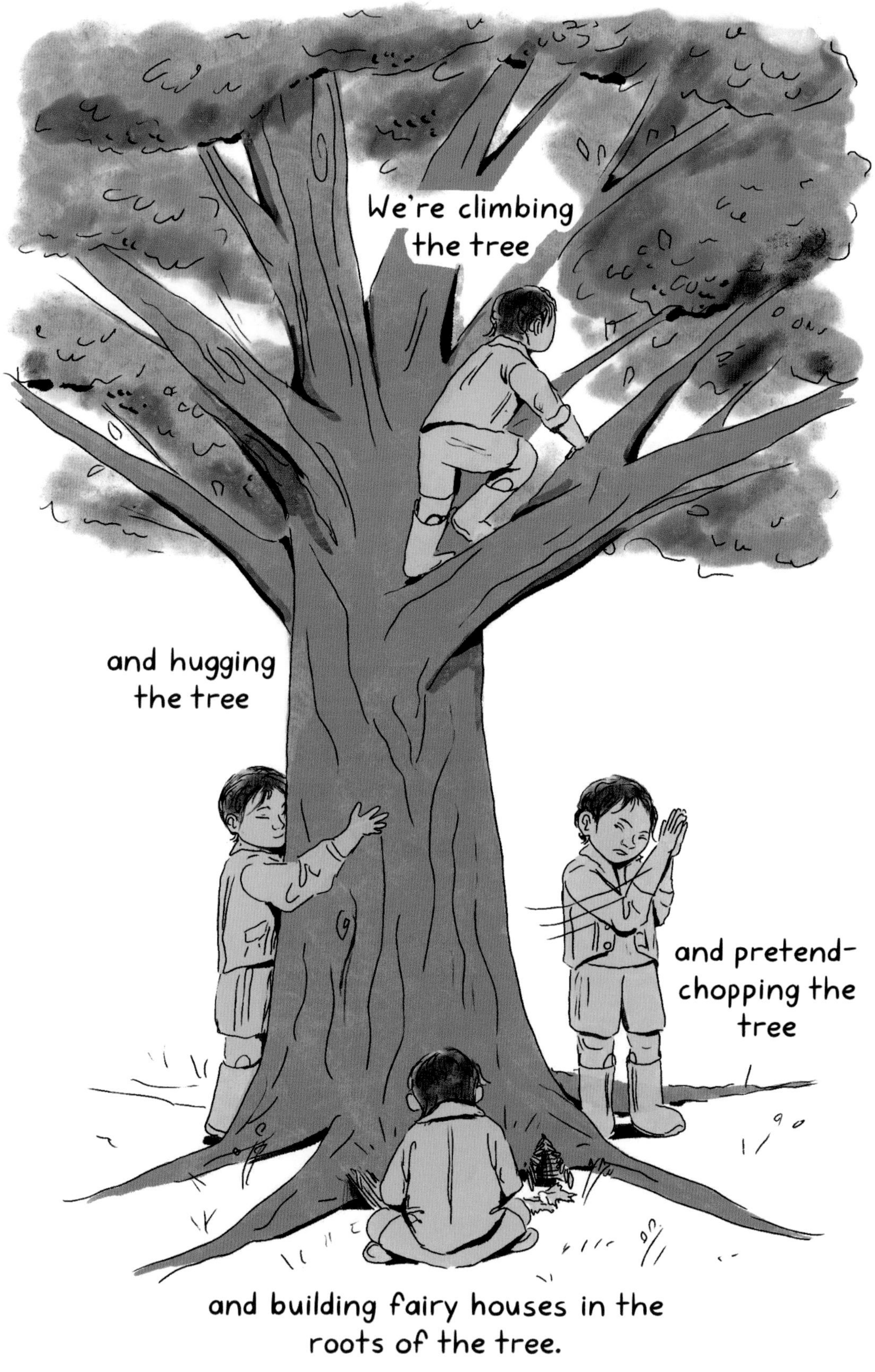
We're climbing the tree
and hugging the tree
and pretend-chopping the tree
and building fairy houses in the roots of the tree.

Let them try everything—at home, at friends' houses, at the drop-in, at preschool, wherever they encounter something to try. Let them play as they prefer, regardless of how it maps onto their presumed gender,

which means if your son just wants to dress all the baby dolls in pajamas and put them to bed, that is fine,

and if your daughter wants to, that is also fine.

The goal is not to produce any particular gender expression, but to empower kids with the freedom to feel that their gender expression is completely up to them.

You can express your values

(no war toys was a choice we made,

and also no clothes with gendered messages on them),

but overall, there are versions of basically everything that you can probably stand to have in the house.

An issue you may experience is that people will say ridiculous things about your choices and/or your children's choices. Some of these will be expected, like

GIRLS CAN'T CLIMB TREES

or

IF YOU LET HIM CARRY THAT DOLL EVERYWHERE, HE'LL GROW UP GAY

and some of them will be so wild you could never have imagined them, like when a woman turned around in line at the bank, stopped short, looked at me accusatorily, and said,

WELL? IS IT A BOY OR A GIRL? THE WAY YOU HAVE IT DRESSED THERE'S NO WAY TO TELL.

These people are exhausting, but they're everywhere, so I recommend you prepare some responses in advance. I don't mind a solid middle finger, but you can also try more reasonable options related to your particular circumstances.

My smart friend Helen Hargreaves, who is a child and family therapist, said something to me once that I have repeated often in these situations:

PLAY IS HOW CHILDREN COMMUNICATE, AND EVERY KIND OF TOY IS A VOCABULARY.

I want my children to have vocabularies of problem solving and nurturing and understanding power and creativity and everything else too.

Or try,

I FIND IT MORE IMPORTANT THAT MY CHILD IS COMFORTABLE AND FEELS EMPOWERED TO PICK WHAT THEY LIKE.

Just be aware that some people, including some people to whom you may be related, will never stop being difficult about this. You may eventually have to make some choices about unsupervised time with these people.

2. There's a bunch more about language.

If you can, persuade your children's teachers to switch to non-gendered language like

FRIENDS or STUDENTS

instead of "boys and girls."

It turns out even doing that really supports a gender-inclusive environment (research from Dr. Rebecca Bigler again). So does ending other gender-segregating practices like boys-against-girls races or challenges or lines, or organizing children in boy-girl-boy-girl order.

In activities:

Address it immediately if a coach or instructor is using gender-shaming or body-shaming language. Some of them don't even necessarily realize that's what they're doing because it's so ingrained,

but if a soccer coach says,

or a dance instructor says,

YOU'RE PLAYING LIKE A BUNCH OF LITTLE GIRLS OUT THERE

YOU DON'T DANCE LIKE A GIRL, YOU MOVE LIKE A LINEBACKER

I will have my kid out of there so fast that the wind of my passing tears the thatch from the rooftops.

Yes, this requires being present while the activities are taking place and, when they're older, talking to your children about what kind of language you do and don't find acceptable.

When talking about bodies:

I love the word "most."
As in,

MOST BOYS HAVE PENISES

MOST GIRLS HAVE A VULVA AND A VAGINA

MOST PEOPLE WHO GROW BREASTS ARE GIRLS

Not only does this leave room for valuing trans and non-binary people's bodies, it also gives you an opportunity to open up a space for awareness around other kids who are intersex, especially as there are fewer non-consensual surgeries being done on intersex children, thank goodness.

When someone you know changes their name or pronouns:

Take it seriously and support each other in getting this right. Talk about it with your children as an important way of respecting someone, and remind each other that even if it feels challenging at first, it's worth it.

WE'RE GOING TO VISIT U—

AUNTIE!

—YES, AUNTIE YAEL!

After a couple go-rounds of this,
you'll all be pretty good at it.

SHANA TOVA, AUNTIE!

3. They're very likely to go through a weird little gender essentialist phase starting at about four; do not panic.

Four- to six-year-olds are very excited to categorize things.

Everything.

They are learning rules and how to apply them, and this is when you'll hear the children you raised on a steady diet of gender-expansive messages and trans positivity say,

> GIRLS HAVE LONG HAIR AND BOYS HAVE SHORT HAIR.

> BOYS ARE STRONG AND GIRLS ARE WEAK.

They will say this even if they are a girl with short hair who can run a mile uphill without breathing hard.

Don't worry (or at least, worry quietly).
Just keep gently countering these messages.

BUT GRANDMA JUDY HAS SHORT HAIR, AND SHE'S A GIRL.

AND PASKAL IN YOUR SCOUT TROOP HAS LONG HAIR, AND HE'S A BOY.

SO MAYBE THAT'S NOT TRUE FOR EVERYONE?

They will agree that this is true, and then two days later
you'll have to do it again. It's fine, do not stress;
keep your messages consistent to your values,
and they will move through this.

④ Do gender neutral without the femmephobia.

To be clear, I am all in favour of de-gendering things. But I do notice that some of the staunchest "gender-neutral parenting" people are fine with jeans and T-shirts but not with sundresses. They're happy about dump trucks but not about nail polish.

I think there's a difficult undercurrent in gender-neutral parenting that leans strongly toward the "masculine lite" and reproduces a certain lobe of sexism as it does so. I also think it's very hard to notice when this is happening because we like the idea of gender-neutral things, but few things are actually really gender neutral in this modern moment. The best we can do, I think, is aim for a rough balance, as in the Zoom Out chapter, but please keep an eye on making sure that your balance includes opportunities for glitter and ruffles and sequins, which are also great for people of all genders if they choose them.

5. Make sure you talk about sexism and how it impacts gender.

Because our culture values masculinity, we accept girls who are "boyish" more readily than boys who are "girly," because the girls are seen as doing something more valuable and the boys are seen as making themselves less valuable.

You can push back against this by making sure that your gender messaging includes not just "girl power" but also validation that boys can be nurturing, express their emotions, and show caring and tenderness (and again, that non-binary people exist between, beyond, or in opposition to the gender binary, and their experiences can be intensely impacted by their gender expression—they won't all be the same).

Name this explicitly with your children as they get older so they know what they're looking at when they observe that gender noncompliance is received differently depending on a person's assigned sex at birth.

6. If you have a trans or non-binary kid...

Let them lead. That's all.

When your kid tells you something important about their gender, ask them what that means to them and what they would like you to do about it, and then, generally speaking, do your best to do that.

There are a million books about raising your trans child that get into the advocacy that awaits you and the feelings you may have, but if we're just doing Greatest Hits of Parenting and Gender, Vol. 1? This song is called "Let Your Kid Lead."

1. Yes, And
2. Language
3. Your Bioessentialist Toddler
4. Degendered Sparkles
5. Gender and Sexism
6. Let Your Kid Lead

Greatest Hits of PARENTING & GENDER Vol. 1

Let them be the expert in their own experience and share it with you—and again, protect their peace about it, which means supporting them in expressing their gender as they wish to.

NOTE:
That includes school, house of worship, activities, and so on if they feel keen— not just at home or in private.

Don't try to talk them out of their gender or suggest that they don't really feel the way they say, and definitely don't tell them you think it's a phase. If they are experimenting with some interesting genders, let them do that with your support until they feel they have arrived at the most correct place for them;

don't set up a situation where they feel like they need to prove to you it wasn't a phase.

To finish, I will quote my brilliant husband, Dr. j wallace skelton, whom I believe is right about many things, including this:

ALL CONVERSATION ABOUT GENDER IS ABOUT LOVING AND SUPPORTING A PERSON AS THEY ARE RIGHT NOW. YOU CAN'T DO HARM TO A PERSON BY BELIEVING THEM ABOUT WHO THEY ARE.

7. Gender also really impacts parenting tasks, way more than you hope it will, good grief.

Rough spots will crop up when you have more, fewer, or different genders of parents than a person or an institution expects. Some people who are accustomed to calling or emailing a mom to talk about a parenting thing can get irrevocably stuck when there's no mom (or two moms) to call or email,

and you will have to gently coach them and also sometimes just pass the incoming message to the correct parent

(the intensity of this really ramps up when school starts and you have less ongoing contact with both the school and the other parents).

For a variety of reasons, including but not limited to sexism and heteronormativity, there are certain expectations in the larger world about which parent will handle which tasks. This is true no matter how many parents a child has or what the genders of those parents are, and if you are not a two-person heterosexual partnership? Parenting will deliver you a lifetime of opportunities to have to explain your family structure and why the "expected" parent isn't going to be handling whatever someone wishes to address to them.

This is true with

medical professionals,

education professionals,

customs and border security officers and other agents of the state's authority,

recreation leaders,

random people behind you in line,

parents of your kids' friends,

camp counsellors,

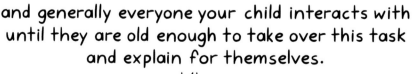

and generally everyone your child interacts with until they are old enough to take over this task and explain for themselves.
Whee.

If you are a couple, and especially if you are read as being heterosexual, people will persist in trying to assign you tasks based on their ideas of what gender of parent should do which things,

and they may be confused or upset or intensely resistant when you ask them to respect your parenting portfolios by saying things like

PLEASE CALL JI-YOO IF RIFA NEEDS TO BE PICKED UP DURING THE DAY, AS FAWZIA IS USUALLY UNAVAILABLE.

Which... sometimes works? But mostly results in years of trying to teach school administrators, camp counsellors, and recreation leaders this lesson. The truth is that even if you do everything up to and including draw a diagram and sing a song about it,

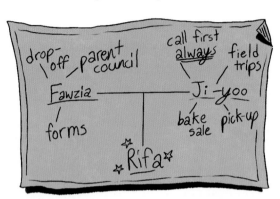

some people will persist in calling a child's mother to ask for her forgotten lunch to be brought to school, even if Ji-yoo is a painter who works from home all day and Fawzia is a trauma surgeon who is currently sewing someone's arm back on,

until your child is old enough to clearly articulate

They will assume that the mom packs the lunches

and the dad coaches the sports teams,

that a mom will know whether a pair of barely worn size 3 boots someone grew out of overnight will be useful and that a dad would have no idea,

etc., ad nauseum, until you are actually nauseated.

Friends may do this, and your parents or other relatives may try to give you a raft of shit about any ways you are not engaging in gendered parenting tasks the way they did. People will even do this when they perceive that one person in a same-sex couple is more femme and one is more butch, because the cisheteropatriarchy is just exhausting.

The only good news here is that the more people jam up its works, the slower it grinds against us all.

19

Strong opinions:

Safety and security.

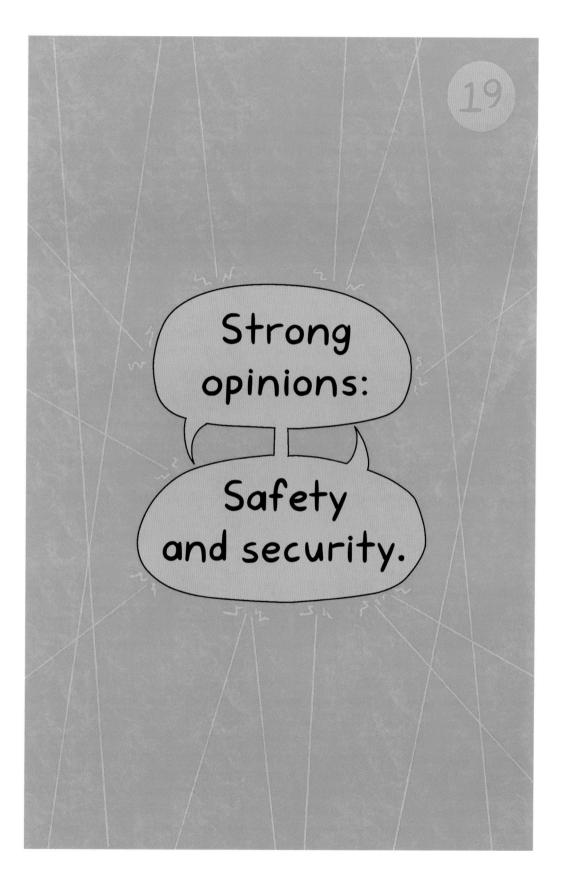

Being the External Risk Management Engine for another person is complicated. It starts with them being at constant risk of injury or death if you don't keep very careful track of literally everything,

but then somehow you have to figure out how and when to hand over each piece of the portfolio for them to manage themselves, and that is terrifying.

On the other hand, a zero-risk childhood isn't possible, nor is it desirable.

Let them try reasonable things, as much as you can stand, so they gain confidence and learn to regroup after a failure or injury.

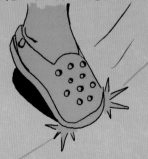

I am not a fan of the "stranger danger" narrative, in which kids are taught never to speak to anyone they don't know. I dislike it for two reasons:

1) This gets really confusing for kids when there's a new person you <u>want</u> them to speak to, whether it's a store clerk or a new colleague or an old friend of yours, and

2) It denies them the opportunity to vibe out who they feel comfortable with and who they don't.

Instead, we say

DON'T <u>GO</u> ANYWHERE WITH A STRANGER, EVER, UNLESS YOU HAVE PERMISSION FROM ONE OF US, SPECIFICALLY, RIGHT THEN.

Also, statistically and so dishearteningly, children are in the most danger from people they already know. For that reason, we talk about the difference between

a secret

and a surprise,

(SOMETHING YOU'RE NEVER SUPPOSED TO TELL)

(SOMETHING YOU CAN'T TELL FOR A LITTLE WHILE SO YOU CAN REVEAL IT WHEN IT WILL BE MOST PLEASING)

We also tell our children that no one, no matter how much we love that person or how much fun they are, should ever ask them to keep something a secret from us, and if they do, to come and let us know immediately.

Bright colours are your friend, especially in winter jackets and swimwear.

Safety orange, neon pink, optic yellow that makes your eyes water a little just to look at it?

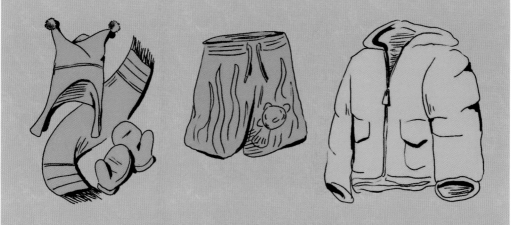

Absolutely yes.
When you lose track of them for a second,
you will thank me for this.

If you still can't find them,
yell out what they're wearing—

SIX-YEAR-OLD,
RAINBOW T-SHIRT,
PURPLE SHORTS!

—and keep yelling it.
Other parents will also pick up your cry
and echo it until some other adult yells,

OVER
HERE!

where you will find your child, unbothered, completely
absorbed in pouring water into their shoes, not listening
to anything else in the world except the little song they
are humming as they do.

Teach them to handle knives, fire, social media, cars, and alcohol safely, under your supervision first, before they're let loose to use them on their own.

Show them how,   supervise them while they try,

make them demonstrate that they know what they're doing (including, especially, what to do if they make a mistake),

and then let them have matches or Instagram.

What to do when you've
fucked up (and you will).

You think it's never going to happen to you, but it probably will. You will promise yourself <u>absolutely</u> that you will never ever scream furiously at your children, and then you do.

Or you'll grab them too roughly,

or you'll overreact and say or do something so unkind.

I've had two of these moments: once I smashed the little flashlight toy a child had gotten at a party into tiny bits, and once I grabbed an ice cream sundae right out of my child's hands while they were eating it in the back seat of the car and threw it as hard as I could into an open field.

Both were terrible out-of-control moments I deeply regret.

Or you won't give them the support they need when they need it the most,

and then you will understand, hopefully not too much later,

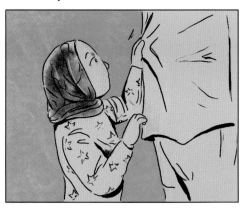

how much you hurt them when you denied them your protection.

You will do them some injury, in body or spirit.

You can't imagine how much your buttons will get pushed in parenting.

You can't imagine how difficult it is when you have been working so hard to be

and it certainly feels to you that no one else in the situation is working hard or even at all.

Your own traumas and fears will roar forward, teeth and claws dripping.

You will be maxed out and stressed out and sleep deprived sometimes, no matter where you set the bar of what is acceptable for you as a parent and what is not.

You will carefully determine your values in parenting,

you will set good and thoughtful rules
for yourself as a parent,

you will do the work to live up to them;

and it's extremely likely the day will come when you'll be about a mile past the end of your own rope, and you will break one of those good and useful rules.

And then you will feel like shit about it.

That's appropriate.

Feeling terrible about it helps you take action
not to repeat it.

You can use your guilt to help you do better
next time.

But the other thing you need to do is apologize.

It's not weak to apologize to your children.
They will not lose respect for you.

Your family is not the army,
and you are not some sort of commander.

You are a leader, and you can and should lead by example. You should go and make amends, you should use this valuable opportunity to say,

> I FELT UPSET AND OVERWHELMED AND I LOST MY TEMPER, AND I AM SORRY. I SHOULD HAVE TAKEN A TIME OUT TO CALM DOWN BUT I DIDN'T, AND THAT WAS WRONG.

You can say,

> I KNOW I HURT YOUR FEELINGS, AND THAT'S NEVER SOMETHING I WANT TO DO. I WILL COMMIT TO LISTENING TO YOU MORE CAREFULLY, EVEN WHEN I AM ALREADY UPSET.

You can say,

> YOU DESERVE BETTER PARENTING FROM ME.

You can say,

> NO ONE SHOULD EVER SPEAK TO YOU LIKE THAT.

And then, you have to make good on your word.

You have to take the moment to calm down, or get settled, or be present, or listen more.

Keep adding to your strategies. It's very likely that your child will forgive you if this doesn't happen very often, but the apology is still critical— for both of you. These too are beautiful moments of parenting grace: the moment of understanding how much this person trusts you and loves you even though you acted like an entire asshole.

But my experience has been: you didn't build it in a day, and you can't break it in a day either, if you apologize and make repair.

It can feel very hard to know that you caused your child harm or fear or loss as a parent. It's a job where you're operating beyond your capacity a lot of the time, and fuck-ups are inevitable. Apologize from the heart and don't make excuses for yourself—make repair, and keep going. There's certainly plenty to do.

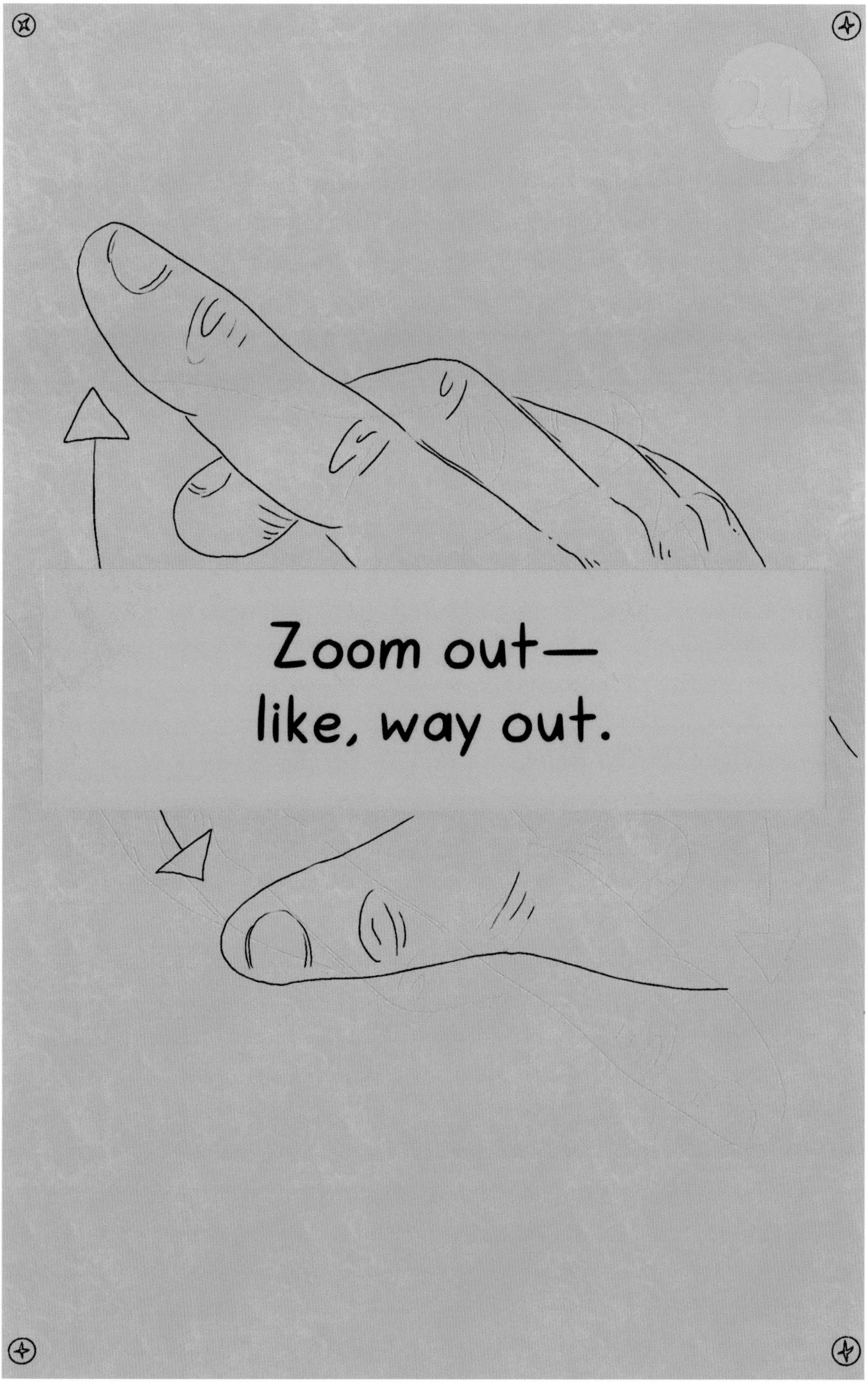
Zoom out—
like, way out.

There is an exceptional amount of conversation about how much of everything children should get in a day, much of it complete with diagrams, charts, and graphs, where the "good" things smile winningly at you and the "bad" things have snaggleteeth and grouchy expressions.

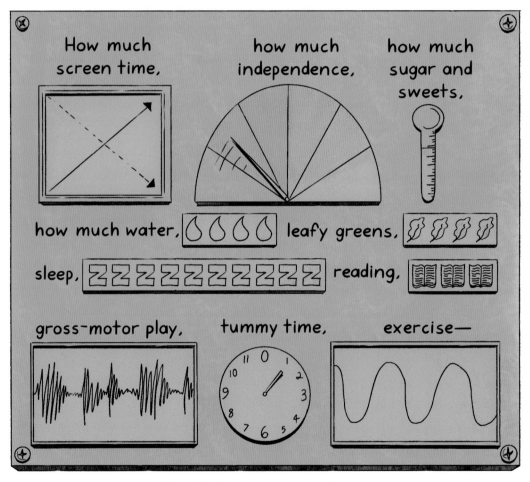

How much screen time, how much independence, how much sugar and sweets, how much water, leafy greens, sleep, reading, gross-motor play, tummy time, exercise—

the list goes on and on.

While sometimes interesting and very occasionally useful,
I find it helpful to think of this discussion in much the
same way I now think of my many preparatory
conversations with the child I didn't yet have:
an exercise that will crumple immediately upon
contact with actual children.

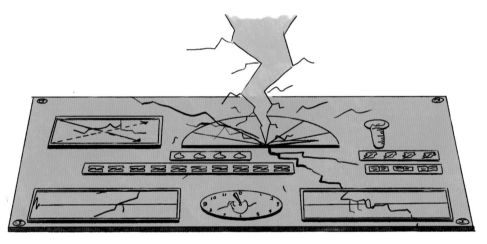

The truth is, friends: parenting is not done in one day.

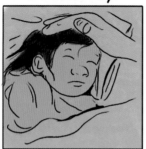

We do not parent a brand-new child each morning.

We have the same ones, Gd willing, for quite some time in a row.

It's a lot of days.

My fear is that all the conversation about recommended daily allowances for this, that, and the other means that some parents, especially new parents, are convinced that each of these things must be accomplished or avoided or facilitated every single day, without fail.

Honey, no.

In order to enjoy parenting,
you have to zoom out.

Children are very not into balance or linearity.

One day they will eat eleven servings of fruit and vegetables, including all the roasted cauliflower you were planning to have for lunch tomorrow,

and the next day absolutely nothing qualifies as a food but Triscuits and gummy sharks.

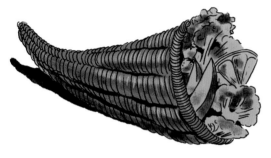

One day all they want to do is draw elaborate mazes and listen to Billy Strayhorn on repeat,

the next day it's eleventy-seven consecutive hours in the pool or on the trampoline until you drag them away, still wailing for just five more minutes,

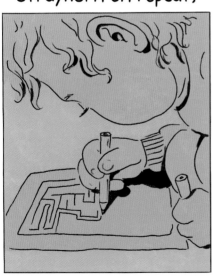

and two days later it's only <u>Moana</u>, all day, until you feel like if you were to meet Dwayne "the Rock" Johnson in person, you might attempt to duct tape his mouth closed, lest he speak to you in his distinctive voice and push you right over the edge.

One day they cheerfully accept and drink from their water bottle every time you hand it to them, and the very next day they're cosplaying as a unicorn in a very cute and very sweaty fuzzy unicorn suit your Phi Beta Sigma line brother sent for Christmas and refusing all attempts at hydration, because

Obviously.

Zooming out is your only hope of preserving your mental health.

Take a monthly average,   or even a quarterly one.

Add up three months of sleep and divide by ninety, and you're probably close to the recommended ten hours per night.

Halloween "bedtime"	+	Early night after swimming	=	Probably fine

Now do the same with everything else.
Otherwise, you'll miss beautiful exceptions—or worse, beat yourself up about them—because you were so worried about everyone's protein intake that you forgot about joy.

Would I serve my children doughnut ice cream sandwiches for breakfast every morning? No.
But on one hot morning in July, when we're on the road and it looks so good, and we won't be here later when it's a more reasonable doughnut-ice-cream-sandwich time?

Absolutely.

Will I let them stay up until midnight to take a nighttime tour of the zoo to see the nocturnal animals out and active, even if it cuts into their sleep and they will probably be utter crabcakes tomorrow?

For sure.

Am I making everyone's bedtime midnight going forward?

Not on your life.
But if I don't zoom out, then I miss these occasions of delight, because they're crowded out by the protein numbers or the sleep goals.

This also applies to other values.
Is there a position somewhere in between

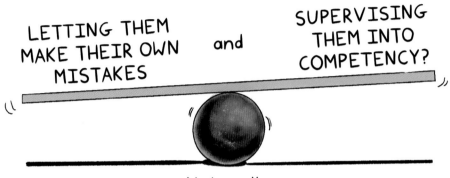

LETTING THEM
MAKE THEIR OWN
MISTAKES
   and
SUPERVISING
THEM INTO
COMPETENCY?

Not really.
The zoom-out method allows you to step back sometimes
and step in sometimes, depending on everyone's energy and
mood and level of resilience in the moment.

You won't always be able to find a middle ground in a
single instance, and so the middle ground becomes
time—how many mistakes can your personal, particular
child make and recover from before they get demoralized
or before you lose your patience with managing the
consequences?

Whether it's one an hour or one a week, start there and
work on slowly growing your capacities together.

Also, not for nothing, day-by-day imperatives are exhausting and demoralizing.
Parenting is already hard enough without making ourselves feel bad because every day isn't

Letting go of that piece of pressure and taking an average over time accounts for fluctuations and variations in kids, but also in parents. I don't always have the energy to cook the rainbow and work my way through a craft project (and then clean up after both).

If I, as a parent, allow myself to have days when I am only up to doing the care minimum, nothing is harmed.

Today's morning with a one-year-old might be a hot breakfast and reading the Poem of the Day aloud at the table;

tomorrow's might be yogurt and listlessly naming all the people whose faces appear on the digital picture frame, but the child is fed and kept company in both situations.

THERE ARE STARS IN YOUR DARK SIDE BRIGHTER THAN ... SUN PROMISE ME, I CATCH YOUR YOU WILL THROW ... T TO SEA IMMED ...

JEANNIE, MURRAY, LOIS, EVAN, FYFE, AND KIPP... JOHN, GRACE, AND KALERA...

Here it is: there's protein in ice cream.
They can catch up on sleep tomorrow night.
<u>Moana</u> is fine;

so is <u>Moana</u> five
times in a row
(headphones are also
very good).

Not every single day, but sometimes? Sure.

You're not a good parent the day they eat hummus and vegetables for lunch

and a bad parent the day lunch is a slice of pizza from Target in the back of the car.

You're a good parent every day you feed them,

every day you tuck them in and kiss them,

every day you know what they did during the day and how they felt about it,

...AND THEN AT RECESS WE HID IN THE LEAVES...

or even just every day you ended up with the same number of children you started with and in roughly the same condition.

Zoom out. You're doing fine.

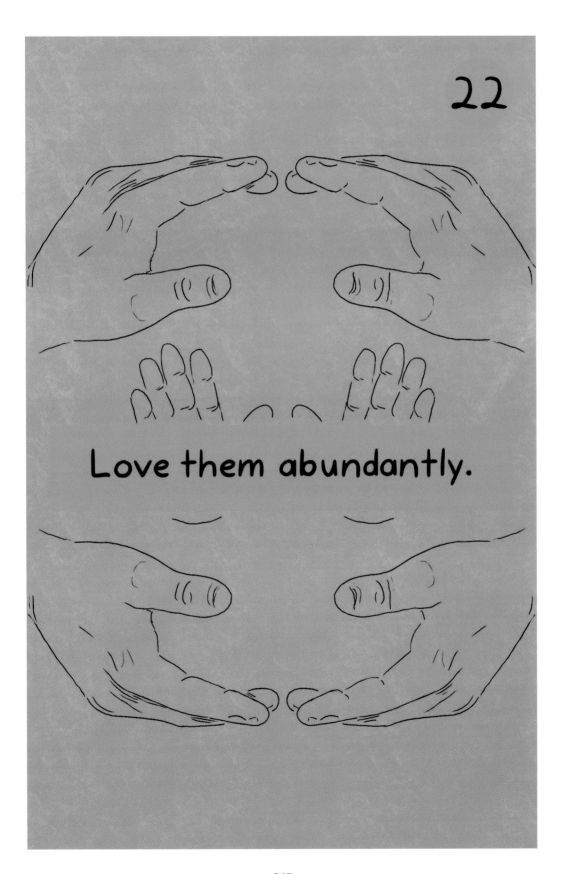

Love them abundantly.

Pick them up every time they cry,
even if you think they're too big for
that, and when they truly are too
big to pick up, open your arms and
let them crawl into your lap.

Cover them with kisses.

Tell them you love them every time you say goodbye or good night, but also every time you're thinking it.

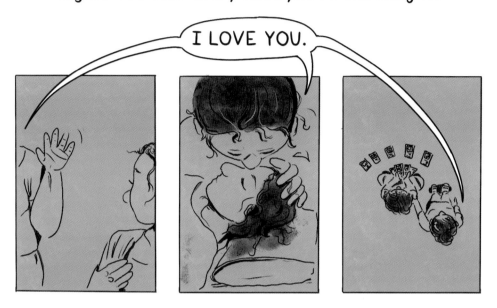

Let them come into bed to cuddle in the mornings as long as they ask to; set your alarm ten minutes earlier so you can tangle your feet up with theirs and murmur together about your dreams.

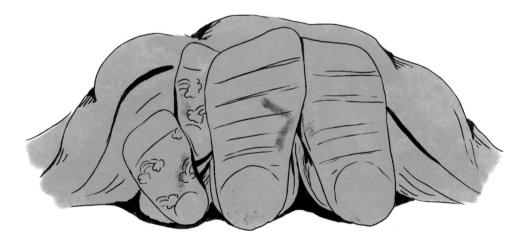

Hold hands even when they can
cross the street on their own.

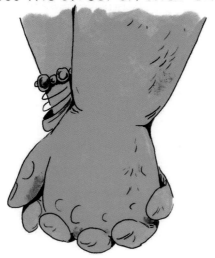

Watch movies leaning on each other; let them put their
heads in your lap and then, after fewer years than you
think, put your head in theirs.

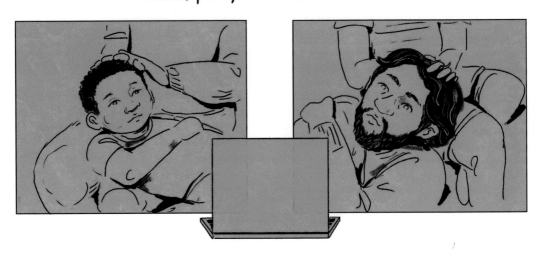

Smooth their hair and kiss them on the tops of their heads for as long as they will stand for it

(and when they say stop or not here, let them draw the boundary and give it your respect).

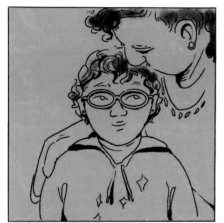

Have pet names and private jokes and little bits you do together.

Let them be the ones to instruct you whenever possible and praise them for it. If you learn a shocking amount about chess or Pokémon or tag variants or baseball along the way, that is also just fine.

Take their hurts seriously, kiss their boo-boos even if you think they might be too old, and when their feelings get hurt, sometimes you just need to have a cookie before dinner about it and try again tomorrow.

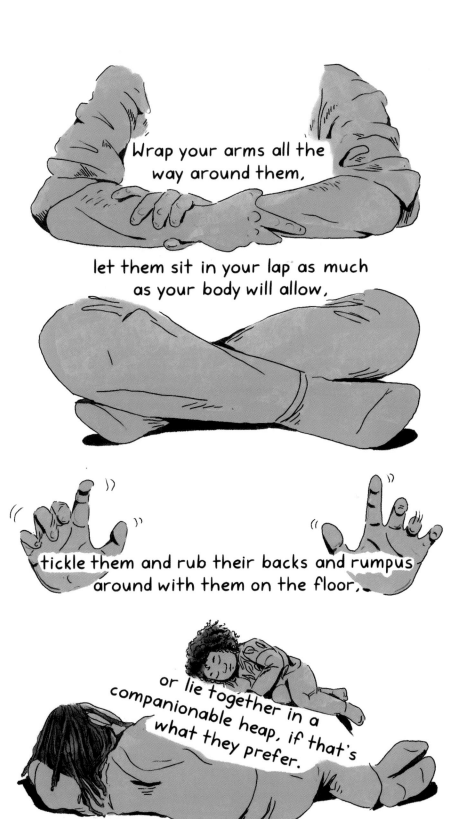

Wrap your arms all the way around them,

let them sit in your lap as much as your body will allow,

tickle them and rub their backs and rumpus around with them on the floor,

or lie together in a companionable heap, if that's what they prefer.

Let the door of your tender affection always be open to them, let them come close and stay there; welcome them into the sanctuary of your embrace at any time,

and then, even when or if there are weeks or months that they refuse your hug as though you've offered to put a damp finger in their ear,

you can know that their refusal is a power you have cultivated and be glad of that as well.

BEAR'S ACKNOWLEDGMENTS

Writing a book remains a weird thing to do, in that you have your thoughts in private and then broadcast them to the entire reading public. Honestly, sometimes I am surprised that people do it at all. In my particular case, for better or for worse (but I hope for better), I am bolstered in my nonsense by a really stellar group of people who have and continue to encourage me, teach me, and call me on my shit. For these invaluable efforts, I am grateful to Angel Adeyoha, Koja Adeyoha, Calvin Anderson, Laura Antoniou, John Austin, Morgan Baskin, Joseph Berman, Hanne Blank, Kate Bornstein, Ivan Coyote, Leigh Ann Craig, Katie Diamond, Lisa Eckstein, the Fairley-Andersens, the Fletcher-Pachecos, Zoë Gemelli, Jennie Gruber, the Hans-Mitchells, the Hargreaves family, Jennifer Heiser, Amber Hollibaugh (who died between when this was finished and when you are holding it and so, in my tradition, we say her name and then zichrono livracha, of blessed memory), Laura Waters Jackson, Mike Jenkins, Victor Kolade, Robert Lawrence, Kris Librera, Zev Lowe, Jonathan Mack, Seth Marnin, the Miracula family, Tori Paulman, Jennifer Peepas, Leah Lakshmi Piepzna-Samarasinha, Morgen Pilon, Carol Queen, Danya Ruttenberg, Abi Salole, Scott Turner Schofield, Jenn Lion Seeley, Michel Sereacki, Eve Shapiro, Peggy Sue, Karen Taylor, Rachel B. Tiven, Syrus Marcus Ware, and Chris Veldhoven. Also to my nana, Barbara Baker, who is about to turn one hundred as of this writing and may yet live long enough to see her name in this book; my parents, Carlyn and Michael Bergman; my brother, Jeff, and his wife, Lisa; my nephews, Levi and Sam Bergman; my uncles, David Bergman and John Lessner; my in-laws, David and Diane Wallace; and my sister-in-law, Bronwen Wallace; as well as the grandparents I had for such a long and lucky time, Bernard Baker z"l, Rita Bergman z"l, and Stanley Bergman z"l.

When I was a tiny queer being in dire need of support and mentorship, I found it in the online community of America Online, a community that eventually moved offline and some of whom remain some of my oldest friends: Bucky Chapell, Chris Leavy, Greg Parkinson, Dave Davis, Deacon Macubbin, Dave Mills, Dorsie Hathaway, Gwen Smith, and Martin Rodriguez-Ema, as well as Will Mura, who died. They supported me while I came out, made a ruckus, and started to figure myself out. I also spent a lot of time at BAGLY drop-in groups and was welcomed every time by the extraordinary Grace Sterling Stowell, a woman aptly named. When I say that I wouldn't have managed without them all, I really mean it.

In the making of this book in particular, great thanks are due to Rachelle Kobilarov, all the amazing humans at Arsenal Pulp Press, the research of Dr. Rebecca Bigler, and the writing of Dr. Rudine Sims Bishop, Po Bronson, Ta-Nehisi Coates, bell hooks, Ashley Merriman, and Imani Perry. I read widely as I thought about how to write about parenting, and the things I read ranged from pleasing to truly nauseating, but those are the writers whose work ushered me into new vistas of ideas.

Saul Freedman-Lawson, illustrator extraordinaire, continued to improve and embellish my advice with his artwork and pushed me to write better and more vivid words so he could have some fun in the drawings. I deeply appreciate his creative partnership and thoughtfulness, in addition to his incredible talent. I remain honoured by the fact that he thinks my words are worth his pictures.

My husband, co-parent, partner, and sweetest sweetheart, j wallace skelton, deserves deeper, broader, and more enduring thanks than an acknowledgments page can possibly provide. I cannot imagine a better person to parent with, nor a more thoughtful editor as I worked my way slowly through trying to imagine what to include, what to cut, and how to explain things. Sixteen years along, what I know for sure is that anything I write is better if he's had a pass at it too, any idea is more robust if I've kicked it around with him first, and any project is more fun when we can work on it together.

And thanks to my children, Morgan, Shir, and Solomon, who contributed considerably to any wisdom you might find in this book and who have put up with so much of my bullshit. It's a great gift to not only love your children but also genuinely like them, and I like all of them very much (even at the end of weeks together on the road).

Thank you to Francis for all his dogly offices, a great comfort to me.

SAUL'S ACKNOWLEDGMENTS

I am grateful to Brian Lam, Catharine Chen, JC Cham, Erin Chan, Cynara Geissler, and Jazmin Welch at Arsenal Pulp Press, for your support and patience in making this book.

Throughout the process of working on *Special Topics in Being a Parent*, I spent time with the work of Lee Lai, Catherine Opie, Mary Kelly, Shira Spector, micha cárdenas, and Alexis Pauline Gumbs. I am honoured to learn from and admire their art and writing.

Thank you to the friends whose care and company made this book possible. I am especially grateful to Vivien Illion, James Rabinovich, Alexandra Siklos, and (as an editor as well as a friend) A. Light Zachary. Many of these pages were drawn in and improved by your company.

Thank you, always, even in the complications, to the people and places that helped raise me. First and foremost to my parents, and also to my shul, Machane Lev, *Shameless* magazine, Lani Freedman, j wallace skelton, and S. Bear Bergman.

Thank you to the younger-than-me people whose childhoods I was or am privileged to be a part of: to my brothers, Ashey and JoJo; to Shir and Solomon Bergman; to all of my campers and students, and to other children I have cared for and learned from.

Thank you again to S. Bear Bergman. I am grateful for the ways you welcome children to the world and welcome adults to do better within that world, grateful to learn from you, grateful to create and build with you again.

S. BEAR BERGMAN is a writer, storyteller, activist, and the founder and publisher of Flamingo Rampant, which makes feminist, culturally diverse children's picture books about LGBTQ2S+ kids and families. He writes creative non-fiction for grown-ups, fiction for children, resolutely factual features for various publications, and the advice column Asking Bear. His books include *The Nearest Exit May Be Behind You* and *Blood, Marriage, Wine & Glitter*, and he was the co-editor with Kate Bornstein of *Gender Outlaws: The Next Generation*.

sbearbergman.com | askingbear.com

SAUL FREEDMAN-LAWSON is an artist, bookseller, and camp counsellor living and working in Toronto. They are the illustrator of *Special Topics in Being a Human* and *Special Topics in Being a Parent*.

sfreedmanlawson.com